RACISM
REVENGE
AND RUIN

RACISM
REVENGE
AND RUIN

It's ALL Obama

SCOTT MCKAY

Published by

The Calamo Press
Washington D.C.

calamopress.com
Currente-Calamo LLC
2425 17th St NW, Washington D.C. 20009
© Copyright by Scott McKay
All rights reserved

Hardcover ISBN: 978-1-958682-06-7
Ebook ISBN: 978-1-958682-07-4

Printed in Canada

To the America we love,
in the devout hope she will reclaim herself

PREFACE

Barack Obama left the Oval Office on January 20, 2017, but he is not part of America's past. He is our present. And our future.

Indeed, the man's malignant influence on the country is stronger today than ever. So powerful is the gravitational force he exerts over the Democratic Party, so fully have the qualities he embodies been subsumed within its DNA – the casting of political foes as morally repellant; the weaponization of government for nakedly partisan ends; the unveiled contempt for America itself – that for the foreseeable future the identity of other Democrat figureheads will be almost incidental. As Obama and his minions have presided over the puppet presidency of Joe Biden, so, under whatever soulless "leader," they will continue to tear away at the values and traditions that are the bedrock of the nation's greatness.

Obama remains in place even physically, the only ex-president aside from the dying Woodrow Wilson to resolutely remain in Washington, D.C.

True enough, by traditional measures Obama is easily dismissed as an all-style-no-substance lightweight – vacuous, inept and short-sighted domestically, indecisive and badly overmatched on the world stage. While he never ceased setting liberal hearts aflutter as, in Biden's revealing characterization, "the first mainstream African-American who is articulate and bright and clean and a nice-looking guy," by every standard measure, in policy terms he was an abject failure.

i

But what dawned on too many far too late is that his objectives were never those of a conventional politician, let alone those of his predecessors in the White House.

They were those of a committed leftist, spruced up for public consumption but paralleling those of our nation's vilest and most intractable longtime foes.

In the bitter and chaotic present, many wonder how America seemingly changed overnight. How did we go from a proud, diverse people living in relative harmony to a self-hating collection of grievance-driven tribes?

How did it happen, as the Cato Institute's Brink Lindsey summed it up, that the "most flamboyantly anti-American rhetoric of 60's radicals is now more or less conventional wisdom among many progressives. America, the land of white supremacy and structural racism and patriarchy, the perpetrator of indigenous displacement and genocide, the world's biggest polluter…?"

How did it happen that, even in the minutia of daily life – from business and medical forms now demanding our pronouns to TV ads all but scrubbed of straight white couples – nothing is as it was?

How did it happen that tens of millions of Americans, including key members of the ruling class, today profess to be unable to define 'woman,' and otherwise prostrate themselves before the lunacy that is transgenderism?

The answer is Barack Obama, who to the extent he was able, made policy out of the left's wish list. And, far worse, used his considerable charm to turn most of entire generations against fundamental beliefs and precepts that had been cherished by every generation since the nation's founding.

Behind the sleek façade, and the soothing bromides about "hope and change," the 44th president was always dedicated to the obliteration of the America we knew. Which is to say, though the onetime community organizer appeared a failure by every conventional standard, he actually succeeded spectacularly in realizing his campaign pledge to "fundamentally transform" America. He remade in his image first his party, and then, institution by institution, the nation itself.

In no way has this shown itself with more devastating effect than in the mounting hostility between the races, and the many other ways the sweeping movements for "social justice" and "equity" have set us at each other's throats. In ways that only yesterday would have been deemed unthinkable – indeed, the antithesis of the American creed – tens of millions have been cast into broad categories of oppressed and oppressor, and the nation itself as "systemically racist."

In today's toxic atmosphere, with fully forty percent of Americans refusing to rule out the possibility of racial civil war, it is startling to be reminded that at the time Obama appeared on the national scene, race relations had never been better. According to a survey taken in 2007, the year he launched his presidential run, three-quarters of Americans, across regional and party lines, recognizing the depth of past injustices, enthusiastically embraced Martin Luther King's vision of a color-blind America. Obama's very election was regarded as ultimate confirmation of the fact. The issue that had bedeviled the nation since its founding seemed at last well on its way to resolution. Instead, it ushered in today's dystopian nightmare.

In innumerable ways, this is no longer the America in which we grew up. It is not the America of JFK, or Ronald Reagan, or even Bill Clinton. Not anymore. Thanks to Obama, so little of that America remains that our young people lack even a rudimentary understanding of what it was – either its greatness, or what made it so.

And entire generations have signed up to crusade against and punish those of us who think otherwise.

Our very freedoms are under siege – starting with our freedom of speech. We've lost the free-market economy which created the most prosperous nation in the world. Instead, we are stultified and strangled economically. Meanwhile, what used to be regarded as deviant counter-culture is every-where mainstreamed and normalized, as the schools, popular culture, the arts, and the news media enforce a constant drumbeat of critical race theory, radical queer and transgen-der ideology, multiculturalism, and moral relativism.

Woe betide the traditional Christian who wants to wear his faith on his sleeve, or publicly proclaim its values in business or the town square – or even to enforce it within the confines of the household. Having made war on public con-science and won, Obama's America is now at war with private conscience, with children often serving as the battleground.

In the political sphere, those cultural aggressions increas-ingly calcify into stone walls of legislation, with radical left-wing policies never tried in thousands of years of civilization ensconced in law as new "civil rights" and clothed in constitutional garb as the traditional majority look on in horror. American exceptionalism is denounced as bigotry while our institutions of power are yoked to a globalist agenda injurious to our interests. Power is concentrated in fewer and fewer hands, and those hands do the work of radicals.

The rule of law hangs by a thread, so selectively enforced – or brazenly flaunted in the targeting of elitist foes – that comparisons to totalitarian states are ever more justified.

Patriotism itself is dying. 70% regarded it as a cherished virtue at the dawn of the 21st Century but now, only 38% do, with no bottom in sight. The young, especially, loathe America, and increasingly have no hesitation proclaiming so.

Obama led and guided these changes, and he promotes them still. None of it is accidental.

TABLE OF CONTENTS

CHAPTER 1
He's Still In Charge..1

CHAPTER 2
From the Start, Built on Lies.....................................19

CHAPTER 3
Red Diaper Baby...35

CHAPTER 4
Dreams From the Guy Who Lives in My Neighborhood.....63

CHAPTER 5
Organizing For American Ruin...................................75

CHAPTER 6
Ridin' Dirty..85

CHAPTER 7
The Magic Negro...103

CHAPTER 8
Critical Race Theory and the Woke Mind Virus..........119

CHAPTER 9
The Bait and Switch...131

CHAPTER 10
Obama's Enemies List: Half of America......................143

CHAPTER 11
Apologizing For Greatness...157

CHAPTER 12
Economic Fascism...173

CHAPTER 13
Racial Pyromania 191

CHAPTER 14
Anti-Cop, Pro-Criminal 203

CHAPTER 15
The War on Faith 217

CHAPTER 16
Obama's Red Guard 229

CHAPTER 17
The Undermining of Donald Trump 243

CHAPTER 18
Please, No, No Fifth Term! 285

CHAPTER 1

HE'S STILL IN CHARGE

On April 15, 2022, Barack Obama visited the White House for the first time in more than five years, and what is most telling is what it showed about his supposed successor.

To say Obama was welcomed like a conquering hero hardly does the extraordinary scene justice. Surrounded by gleeful White House staff and invited Democrat pols, he was like an emperor, honoring his adoring subjects with his mere presence, offering a word to this one, a smiling nod to that one, a touch of the royal hand to the next.

Make that, an emperor/rock star, since the women among the invited guests — think Senator Amy Klobuchar (D-Minn.) and an even-giddier than-usual Kamala Harris — mobbed him like young girls at a Harry Styles concert.

The purported president? In the video of the event, Joe Biden can be seen wandering at the edge of the throng, trying, and failing, to catch Obama's notice, before wandering off, vacant-eyed. When Obama finally deigns to acknowledge his presence, Biden exults in this, saying seeing him "brings back so many good memories." Then, in his eagerness to please, he refers to himself as "Joe Biden, Barack Obama's vice president."

Less kindly, Obama responds by calling him "Vice President Biden," before smirking and saying, "That was a joke."

When the video went viral, even Democrats recalled Obama's assessment of the sitting president – "Don't underestimate Joe's ability to fuck things up" – and only then did Obama tweet some mild pretend respect for his successor. "Always great catching up with @POTUS. Thanks for all you're doing to help even more Americans get access to quality, affordable healthcare."

But this wasn't fooling anyone. It was already abundantly clear to millions that Biden's presidency was a sham, and the doddering dunce of a man a mere puppet.

And that the true power in Washington lay not in the White House, but in Barack and Michelle's lavish home in the fashionable Kalorama section of town.

In fact, Biden administration officials are scarcely attempting to hide the truth. "It has been an honor and privilege," as retiring Biden press secretary Jen Psaki let it slip on *The View*, "...working for President Obama," before hastily correcting herself.

"So today," chimed in her hapless successor, Karine Jean-Pierre, not long after, "just as you all saw, President Obama announced..." The house-trained press merely snickered.

Of course, in no way is it more glaringly obvious who is calling the shots than in that the identities of those occupying the Biden administration's highest echelons. The Obama flunkies were back in a rush.

Biden's first chief of staff, Ron Klain, an Obama minion who never quite made the first string, set the tone from Day One. Having served as VP Biden's chief of staff from 2009-11, and before that as chief counsel for the Senate Judiciary Committee, he'd played a lead role in orchestrating the shameful circus that was Clarence Thomas' Supreme Court confirmation hearing. Klain was thus well-versed in racial pandering at its most loathsome. Thus, he was now positioned to revive at the highest level a defining Obama reflex, the readiness to shamelessly slander political opponents as bigots. Top heavy as it is with white progressives, always seeking opportunities to parade their anti-white *bona fides* for the benefit of the progressive core woke constituency, the Obama Redux administration has, if anything, indulged that impulse even more cynically than the original.

Like Obama himself, Klain failed upwards, using radical politics as a means for making up for his complicity in disastrous policies. His promotions came after he had served as a lobbyist for Fannie Mae, the quasi-governmental housing lending agency whose policies helped crash the housing market and tanked the U.S. economy in 2008.

Then there's Jake Sullivan, Obama's former director of policy who became Biden's National Security Adviser. Under Obama his tenure was marked by his leading role in not one but three catastrophic Middle East failures: the Syria disaster; the terrorist attack on the U.S. consular facility in Benghazi; and the catastrophic Iran nuclear deal. These marked him as criminally incompetent, if not as an actual criminal. That designation came with his key role on behalf of Team-Obama in perpetrating the Trump-Russia hoax. It began during the 2016 campaign and continues in the ongoing coverup even today. Indeed, over that time no one's fingerprints have been more evident in this viciously corrupt assault on democratic norms than Jake Sullivan's.

It was Sullivan who, just before Election Day 2016, blasted out the false claim that Trump had a "secret hotline" to Russia via Alfa Bank. The supposed "proof" was a computer server inside Trump Tower, which was receiving messages that turned out to be spam emails. Four years later, Sullivan was leading the plot, in concert with now-Secretary of State Anthony Blinken, to drum up "intelligence community professionals" – i.e., mainly fellow Obama stooges like Michael Hayden, Michael Morrell, James Clapper and John Brennan – to sign the letter dismissing the infamous Hunter Biden laptop, with its damning evidence implicating both Hunter and Biden himself in criminal influence peddling as "Russian disinformation." Surveys taken after the election established that more than 10 percent of those who voted for Biden would have voted differently had they known about the damaging information on the laptop.

That the Russia Hoax was orchestrated from the Obama White House has of course been gallingly obvious to everyone, even as the legacy media has studiously refused to acknowledge the fact. But with the long-delayed release of the Durham Report in May 2023, there seemed reason to hope even Democrats would at last have to admit the truth.

"Durham's damning conclusion must never be forgotten," as veteran newspaper columnist Michael Goodwin summed it up on May 16. "We now know, without doubt, that Barack Obama's Justice Department and officials from other parts of the government meddled in the election and tried to pick the president regardless of the wishes of 130 million voters."

"What did he know and when did he know it?" That was the question asked of Richard Nixon at the height of the Watergate scandal. In Obama's case, thanks to the Durham Report, we know for sure: August 3, 2016, when CIA Director Brennan briefed Obama on Hillary Clinton's operation "to vilify Donald Trump by stirring up a scandal claiming interference by the Russian security services."

"Obama knew what was going on and so did his vice president, Joe Biden," as Michael Goodwin puts it. "That, too, is now settled forever."

Forty indictments came in the wake of Watergate, and several of Nixon's top advisors did serious jail time. But no such luck – not with Obama and his minions still running things. For their roles in an infinitely more consequential breach of both law and public trust, Jake Sullivan and Anthony Blinken got plum jobs in the Biden/Obama regime, and they remain in place, wholly untroubled by a compliant media.

Indeed, in his new job, Sullivan was soon adding to his reputation as a foreign policy Typhoid Mary, with his lead performance engineering the debacle that was America's disastrous Afghanistan pullout. Needless to say, the widespread calls that followed for his resignation were ignored.

Samantha Power, another embarrassment under Obama as the architect of his infamous Apology Tour, has likewise continued to prosper. She is now in charge of distributing billions of dollars in foreign aid, through United States Aid For International Development (USAID) agency, resources bestowed upon regimes that are in accord with globalist views, and withheld from governments – like those of Hungary's Viktor Orban (for standing fast against transgenderism) and Israel's Bibi Netanyahu – that challenge leftist dogma.

Power played a notable role in what remains arguably the key success in the early days of the campaign to destroy the newly elected Trump, when she repeatedly demanded the "unmasking" of General Mike Flynn, Trump's designee for national security advisor. The subsequent "unmasking," in seven surveillance wiretaps, was soon leaked to the *Washington Post*, and proved key to discrediting Flynn, even as it reinforced the building narrative that Trump colluded with Russia to win the election. Ultimately, induced by FBI interrogators into telling a meaningless falsehood, Flynn was convicted of lying to the Bureau. His life was ruined, and the Trump administration was left without its most stalwart defender and best hope of dismantling the weaponized intelligence agencies. Yet subsequent investigations showed that - in not revealing all the minor details of an innocuous conversation with a Russian ambassador - he was following standard diplomatic protocol.

Of course, there are many, many other Obama veterans running through the Biden administration, most likewise owning their careers to the former president. They include Defense Secretary Lloyd Austin, who was in charge of US Central Command in Obama's second term; Treasury Secretary Janet Yellen, who ran the Federal Reserve for Obama; and Biden's climate czar, the obnoxious frequent-private-jet-flying former Secretary of State, John Kerry.

Then there's Alejandro Mayorkas, Obama's onetime Director of United States Citizenship and Immigration Services and deputy Director of Homeland Security (DHS), who as Biden's DHS chief has cavalierly overseen the intentional obliteration of America's Southern border. Among the other horrific consequences of this are the fentanyl deaths of three hundred Americans daily. In a rational world he would be facing a lifetime behind bars.

And needless to say, it was Obama's erstwhile Supreme Court nominee Merrick Garland, who as Biden's attorney general, engineered what history will judge as the most damaging break with American norms of all: the criminal indictment of his sponsor's despised predecessor.

And perhaps the most consequential hire was Susan Rice, Obama's former U.N. ambassador and national security adviser, as the director of the all-important Domestic Policy Council. A fierce Obama loyalist, Rice remains best known as the sacrificial lamb sent out while serving as U.N ambassador to appear on all three major network news broadcasts to blame the September 11, 2012 jihadist attack in Benghazi on a poorly-made YouTube video by a Coptic Christian in California that supposedly inflamed the jihadists by mocking the Prophet Muhammad.

"I was close to President Obama and he was a target," Rice later explained in her memoir, before going for the victim card. "I'm an African American woman. I don't take crap off of people. And I'm confident in my own skin… Putting all that together, put it in a political context of the campaign, and maybe I was an attractive target."

Another explanation, of course, is that she insulted the American people by telling a flat-out lie about what happened in Benghazi, the cause of which likely was a lot more closely related to Obama administration gun-running and meddling in the affairs of a sovereign nation than a YouTube video.

In her latest role, Rice laid out the Biden administration's priorities to a friendly interviewer. "I'll be driving our efforts to ensure that matters of equity and justice are fully incorporated into all that we try to do," she said. That was before Rice was given the job of promoting the DEI agenda in every federal agency, which has quietly had the effect of weaponizing the government against the majority of our citizens.

Trump's Director of National Intelligence Rick Grenell, is among those who regard Rice as the functional behind-the-scenes power in the Biden administration, describing her as "the shadow president."

But, of course, given her relationship with Obama, who is never more than a phone call away, that's basically a matter of semantics. While she abruptly dumped out of the Biden administration in the spring of 2023, nobody seriously believes we've seen the last of Susan Rice.

When the smoothly fork-tongued former Obama flack Jen Psaki, Biden's first press secretary, departed that thankless job for the greener pastures of MSNBC, was it Rice who saw to it that her replacement was Katrine Jean-Pierre? Or was it someone else out of the Obama stable? The answer: it doesn't really matter. What does is that those throughout the administration share a common vision and a common set of standards, which made it all but inevitable that as a black gay woman, notwithstanding her demonstrable ineptitude, Jean-Pierre had all the qualifications necessary.

In short, Obama understands, alas far better than Trump ever did, that personnel *is* policy.

SUSAN RICE	LLOYD AUSTIN	AVRIL HAINES
▼	▼	▼
UN Ambassador 2009-2013, National Security Advisor 2013-2017	Commander, U.S. Central Command, 2013-2016 Director, Joint Staff, 2009-2010	Deputy National Security Advisor, 2015-2017
▼	▼	▼
Director, Domestic Policy Council, 2021-2023	Secretary, Department of Defense, 2021-	Deputy Director, CIA, 2013-2015
		▼
		Director of National Intelligence, 2021-

WILLIAM BURNS	VICTORIA NULAND	JANET YELLEN
▼	▼	▼
Deputy Secretary of State, 2011-2014	Assistant Secretary of State for European and Eurasian Affairs. 2013-2017	Chair, Federal Reserve, 2014-2018
▼	▼	▼
Director, CIA 2021-	Deputy Secretary of State, 2023-	Secretary of the Treasury 2021-

ANTHONY BLINKEN	JAKE SULLIVAN	SAMANTHA POWER
▼	▼	▼
Deputy Secretary of State, 2011-2014	Director of Public Planning, State Department, 2011-2013	UN Ambassador, 2013-2017
▼	▼	▼
Directory, CIA, 2021-	National Security Advisor, 2023	Administrator, USAID, 2021

Indeed, in the wake of the country's transformation via the George Floyd riots and the pandemic, he is today endowed with powers undreamed of when he came into office in 2009. Specifically: the power to regulate the economy, from the energy sector to social spending and tax policy, according to leftist dogma. This is the authority to impose on the entire nation, from kindergarten classrooms to corporate suites, a jaw-droppingly radical social agenda – led by diversity, equity and inclusion policies (DEI), transgenderism, and wholesale suppression of people's freedom to dissent from these ideas. All this has taken place without so much as a murmur from the house-trained Democrat Party.

In short, with Biden as front man in what amounts to Obama's third term, (or fourth, if we count his marshaling of the Deep State during the Trump years), all his transgressive aggressions came roaring back in even more toxic form.

It was clear from the outset, for those willing to see, that as an individual Biden was at once pathetic and noxious: a would-be Xerox of Obama, whose beyond-the-sell-date toner leaves the copy infinitely dimmer than the original. So, it is understandable that the less astute would ascribe the Democratic Party's wholesale capitulation to the radical left on his watch to the obvious incompetence of the bumbling dud in the Oval Office.

After all, Biden often tries to appear in charge. And it is also true that in his prior life, Biden, unlike Obama, was never counted a radical or a racial pyromaniac. In fact, when Biden was a senator, he was just as vile, but often in the opposite direction; a close friend of former Ku Klux Grand Wizard Robert Byrd, he said he opposed school busing because he did not want his children sent into a "racial jungle." Thus, the psychological dissonance of the role he must play now in the administration over which he so uncertainly totters, defending policies that out-Obama even the old Obama – may be partly why the hapless purported moderate tends to get so snappish when challenged. Lacking Obama's smoothness and vast capacity for guile, his resentful tone makes things look even worse. It's all Obama – working through others, but always the same man – and in today's

America, an Obama unleashed, now unaccountable to the voters after a sham election.

As Christopher Rufo and Russell Vought point out, woke ideology has so fully migrated from academia into government that it is "now embedded within the very DNA of the federal bureaucracy." Countless government forms imagine we might be something other than male or female. The military designs combats uniforms for pregnant female soldiers – and responds with confusion and hostility when asked about why. Every federal agency is today committed to "equity plans" that enforce the vilest kinds of racial discrimination, like the $4 billion 2021 program "designed to provide debt relief exclusively to non-white farmers."

The notion that working class whites, as presumed "MAGA Republicans" (and "white supremacists"), are no longer deserving of equal treatment by their government is all but written administration policy. One need look no further than the callous indifference afforded the blue collar community of East Palestine, Ohio in the wake of a devastating February 2023 chemical spill. Biden couldn't be bothered to visit an overwhelmingly white community when it suffered an environmental catastrophe – even when his own supporters repeatedly made the point the town is in a swing state.

Everything that happens in this administration, likely down to the timing of his weekly escapes to his Rehoboth beach estate that somehow came his way on a government salary, is planned and executed by an army of Obama holdovers.

By way of horrific example, there is the executive order Biden signed in February 2023 creating a bureaucracy to guarantee "racial equity" throughout all departments of the federal government. Among its many provisions, points out the Center for Individual Rights, "the <u>order</u> calls for an increase in 'the share of federal contracting dollars awarded to small disadvantaged business (SDBs) by 50 percent by 2025," and otherwise serves to "embed equity into all aspects of Federal decision-making."

Racial "equity", as many on the right (but few liberals) know, is a term used by the radical left to deliberately sow confusion. Unlike "equality," which represents equal opportunity, it demands equal results, regardless of skill level, effort or anything else, and having poisoned education, it is doing the same to institutions throughout the culture, insistently defining people not as individuals, but as members of racial groups. Necessarily, the word "equity" appears 21 times in the executive order that mandates racial quotas in hiring throughout the government and is guaranteed to add to the slag heap of ill feeling and bitterness already so depressingly evident in daily American life. As Biden would put it: *C'mon man, gimme a break!*

Back when Barack Obama was pushing social justice on the streets of Chicago and spending his Sundays in Jeremiah Wright's rabidly anti-white and anti-American church, Biden was palling around with some of the most legendary racists ever to serve in the Senate. That not only includes the previously mentioned Robert Byrd of West Virginia, a former Exalted Cyclops of the KKK, but also Mississippi's James Eastland. -- the same James Eastland who said on the Senate floor during the Second World War that blacks were "physically and morally" incapable of fighting and that one of the principle aims of the war effort was to maintain "white supremacy"; and who later said that the *Brown v. Board of Education* Supreme Court ruling outlawing segregation in schools "destroyed" the constitution and that no one was obliged to obey it. Indeed, Biden's close ties with these and other arch-segregationist senators lasted for decades. Indeed, in his farewell speech on leaving the senate in 2008, Biden made a point of saying how even he was surprised by how "deep" his friendship with a cohort of segregationist and openly racist senators had been; and two years later, giving a eulogy for Byrd, he emphasized what a "close friend" he was, praising him as "the dean of the United States Senate." More remarkably, in the midst of his 2016 presidential campaign, Biden was still publicly reminiscing about Eastland, discussing their shared affection and his regret at Eastland's passing.

Other Biden executive orders, some issued his first day in office, threw open the Southern border, killed the Keystone XL pipeline, and further kneecapped domestic energy production by shutting down federal permitting of oil and gas leases. Combined with Biden's reckless decisions on federal spending, those energy policies led to a sudden, sharp increase in inflation – as most economists had predicted.

On issue after issue, the Obama Redux administration has taken steps far more radical than any that President

Obama took during his eight years in the Oval Office, instituting crushing tyrannies in entirely new ways. Could even the most impassioned radical – say, "education reformer" Bill Ayers – have guessed there would come a day when the FBI (!) would be used to identify and label parents attending school board meetings as "domestic terrorists?" Or that half the country (including blacks with the wrong politics: just ask Larry Elder) would be branded "white supremacists?" Or that when a nominee for the Supreme Court would refuse to provide a definition for the word woman her questioners would be held up as bigots? Or that America's southern border would essentially cease to exist and the federal government would sue the state of Texas for trying to place barriers in the Rio Grande?

Needless to say, the devastating consequences of this last set of policies are hard to overstate. As a result of the Biden Administration's removal of deterrence – many by the 94 executive actions he took on immigration in his first hundred days – an estimated five and a half million more illegal immigrants have entered the country in less than two years, and it is literally anyone's guess how many have crossed since then.

At a hearing after the GOP took back the House in the 2022 elections, Chief Patrol Agent John R. Modlin confirmed the obvious, that illegals caught crossing the border "believed when the administration changed, that the law changed and policy changed and there was an open border."

The question is why? What could possibly be the thinking behind such lunacy?

Until recently, the answer would have been that Obama and the party in his thrall believed the vast influx of soon-to-be-voters would permanently bury the country's formerly white majority beneath an avalanche of Third World immigration and childbirth, thereby guaranteeing a permanent Democratic majority. Yet in recent years that calculation has begun to change somewhat, as Hispanics have proven far more resistant to the lure of the welfare state on offer from their would-be Democrat benefactors than blacks have traditionally been. Indeed, in the 2020 presidential race, the uber-capitalist Trump, flaunting a brand of pro-Americanism repellant to orthodox liberalism, drew nearly forty percent of the Hispanic vote, up eight points from his 2016 run; and Ron DeSantis, in his wipeout of Florida Democrats in 2022, actually won the state's Hispanics by fifteen points.

However, what's never changed for committed leftists – from the Communist Party's heyday in the Thirties, through the era of Ayers and the Weathermen in the Sixties and Seventies, on to Antifa and the BLM today, is the conviction that if capitalist America is to be brought down – the essential first step to bringing on the glorious revolutionary future – it will be brought about by tearing down the existing order and destroying the middle class. Everything, every institution and concept buttressing tradition – family, church, education, patriotism, reverence for shared history – must be leveled so the new society might rise in its place.

This is what Obama learned from a string of ideological mentors early on in his career. Obama has freely acknowledged that he was brought to tears listening to Reverend Wright's rabid sermons, and this is what he peddled as a community organizer. There is no evidence he's ever stopped believing it. To the contrary, it has all but become doctrine in the party he dominates, as leftist politicians of the Obama stripe relentlessly put in place precisely the policies – justice "reform," defunding police – that cause crime to skyrocket and otherwise make life unlivable.

Even more striking, the military is being systematically eviscerated in the bizarre cause of "wokeness," leaving the nation ever more vulnerable in a vicious and predatory world. Starting under Obama and now culminating before our eyes, this sickening project is headed by Bishop Garrison, Senior Advisor to the Secretary of Defense for Human Capital and Diversity, Equity and Inclusion. An Obama administration retread, Garrison is an outspoken Critical Race Theory devotee and unapologetic anti-white racist, who (unironically) defines opposition to these beliefs as *prima facie* evidence of bigotry.

In his view, not only is Trump a racist, but so too is anyone who supports him. "He's dragging a lot of bad actors (misogynist, extremists, other racists) out into the light, normalizing their actions," Garrison declared midway through Trump's term. "If you support the President, you support that. There is no room for nuance with this. There is no more 'but I'm not like that' talk.

"Because you're watching what he says. You're listening to his careful choice of words. And you're still willing to

17

follow him and/or not speak out. So yes, you're very much like that. It's time we all step up….(s)upport for him, a racist, is support for ALL his beliefs."

Unsurprisingly, Garrison sees "white supremacism as the number one threat to the U.S. Military," and the steps he is planning to root it out should terrify any American with even a passing interest in civil liberties. Among other things, Garrison says that he wants the government to "continuously" trawl the social media accounts of military personnel for "extremist and concerning" behavior. The definition for this, of course, can include anything that is critical of Diversity, Equity and Inclusion.

It is a terrible time in this country, a time of hopelessness and despair, and everything the left does, all generated and approved by Obama, daily makes it worse.

Hardly least, the endless measures purportedly aimed at ending racism in fact exacerbate it, as anger and a sense of ill-usage rises among Americans of all races.

This is what comes from Obama's racial pyromania – from Trayvon Martin, and Ferguson to, yes, George Floyd – all taken as confirmation of the lie, to which he wholeheartedly subscribes, that a black man can't get a fair shake in America.

All of this is by intention. For, in the absence of instructions from the doddering current Oval Office occupant, Obama's minions are free to formulate policy as they wish, and Obama guides former colleagues who continue to look to him for direction.

CHAPTER 2

FROM THE START, BUILT ON LIES

O n April 28, 2008, came the last, best hope to save America as we knew it.

Barack Obama's presidential campaign seemed on the verge of collapse.

In the year since he'd announced his candidacy for the Democratic nomination, the telegenic young senator from Illinois had had a startlingly easy ride. He and his team had carefully managed just what the public knew of his origins and beliefs – the most fundamental facts about the background of a candidate for the most powerful office in the world, traditionally covered as a matter of course. Which is to say: already the media were showing themselves his most reliable ally, ready to compromise what remained of their integrity to promote his interests.

This was vital, as Obama and his team well knew. For there were things in his past which would not survive even the most casual vetting.

The media's infatuation with Obama, like that of millions of ordinary Americans, had begun with his electrifying 2004 keynote address to the Democratic National Convention. There, as a then-candidate for the U.S. Senate from Illinois, he proclaimed "there is not a liberal America and a conservative America – there is the United States of America. There is not a black America and a white America and Latino America and Asian America – there is the United States of America."

That he'd spoken those inspiring, seemingly heartfelt words was still all that most Americans knew about Obama nearly four years later – and that the young, first term senator had had the nerve to take on presumptive front runner Hillary Clinton for the Democratic presidential nomination.

But successful in marketing Obama as that speech had been, it reflected nothing like what the man really believed about America or its ethnic and racial divides, which, in point of fact, based on the history, was the opposite of unifying or uplifting. And now that that was sure to come out, and for Team Obama things were spiraling out of control.

Reverend Jeremiah Wright was about to break ranks.

The retiring pastor of Chicago's Trinity United Church of Christ, Wright was a longtime racist firebrand – a practitioner of what he called "the prophetic theology of the black church" and others termed "Black Liberation Theology." Yet for nearly twenty years Wright had been Barack Obama's pastor, the politician listening as he thundered out anti-white racist garbage from the pulpit. "God Bless America?" Wright had raged. "No. God Damn America!" And when America was attacked on 9/11, he'd declared "America's chickens are coming home to roost" for its racism and injustice. Wright demanded redistributive justice – reparations – for the sin of slavery and segregation, and he accused white Republicans of sympathy with the Ku Klux Klan.

And Barack Obama had been there for it all.

The relationship had been beneficial to both men. Obama was clearly a young politico on the rise, with the sorts of media and political connections useful to a man like Wright, and the reverend had lent the mixed-race and polished Obama much needed credibility with the under-class blacks who were his primary constituency. Over the years they'd drawn closer, with Wright increasingly assuming the role of mentor.

But now the sermons – or, more accurately, rants – emanating from Wright's pulpit were looming as a disaster, one that could stop Obama's blossoming candidacy dead in its tracks.

Team Obama had been aware of such a possibility for some time. Indeed, he'd originally planned to have Wright deliver the invocation on the announcement of his candidacy in Springfield, the Illinois state capital – the site chosen to evoke comparisons with the city's greatest resident, Abraham Lincoln – fourteen months earlier, on February 10, 2007.

But shortly before, a devastating piece appeared in, of all places, *Rolling Stone Magazine*. It turned out the rock bible had had a reporter in Wright's church. Worse, there was a recording of the "sermon."

So Wright was gently disinvited from his role in the event, and the campaign began pressuring Wright to moderate himself, lest other journalists might make their way into Obama's church, listening to his longtime pastor. According to Wright, in an interview years later with journalist Ed Klein, there was even an offer of $150,000 if he would go entirely silent through the November election.

Obama and his minions needn't have worried: the press was more than ready to play the role of Praetorian Guard, shielding him at all costs from public release of damaging revelations about his actions and beliefs, past or present.

Without them, he wouldn't have had a chance. Despite his early victories in the Iowa caucuses and South Carolina's primary, the coming months loomed as a fight-to-the-death against Hillary, and in the hands of his ruthless opponent, Reverend Jeremiah Wright stomping through the china shelves would be the instrument of that loss.

Indeed, even as the Wright story was being studiously downplayed by the legacy media, the conservative press was on to it, with Sean Hannity in particular hammering Obama with it almost nightly. So much so that by March 2008 even the most shameless mainstream outlets were finding it hard to ignore completely.

The New York Times finally got around to acknowledging the Obama-Wright connection on March 6 – albeit on page 19, and, as Bernard Goldberg pointed out in his aptly named book on the media's coverage of the campaign, *A Slobbering Love Affair*, "leaving out all the inflammatory specifics about Wright's 'rough sermons' that had already appeared in *Rolling Stone*."

Nonetheless, for Obama, the potential destructive power of even such mealy-mouthed coverage was limitless, so completely did his mentor's vile worldview undermine his own carefully nurtured brand as the ultimate healer, destined by fate to salve the nation's long-festering racial wounds.

Even worse, Reverend Wright seemed poised to personally expose his protégé's supposed moderation for what it was: a cynical fraud.

Obama had no choice but to finally confront the crisis head-on.

The speech he delivered in Philadelphia on March 18, 2008 would be dubbed the "More Perfect Union Speech." According to a Pew survey released a week later, 85% of Americans said they'd heard a little of it, and 54% said they'd heard a lot.

And in a way, it was masterful, deftly playing to America's deep yearning for harmony and racial reconciliation, even as it absolved Obama from any responsibility for his own record.

"The big idea of the speech," as NPR would tell it, "was that to move forward on race, all of America would have to forgive each other and come together. On that theme, there is a section of the speech where Obama compares Reverend Wright, who had said all those incendiary things, to his grandmother," whom he claimed to have heard expressing distrust of aggressive black panhandlers.

Those famous words: "I can no more disown him than I can disown the black community. I can no more disown him than I can disown my white grandmother, a woman who helped raise me..."

It was, in short, designed to not merely make the Wright issue disappear, but to buttress his brand of racial healer, and in this it succeeded brilliantly. All these years later, liberals still get misty eyed talking about it.

But Jeremiah Wright, for one, was appalled. For two decades Obama had sought his counsel, used his contacts, traded on his alliances and soaked up his teachings while building a career first as a Chicago community organizer, then an Illinois state legislator, then as a senator. And Jeremiah Wright had never been a problem for Barack Obama then.

So the following month, on April 28, 2008, addressing the National Press Club as part of the opening of a confab held in Washington, D.C. to celebrate the history of the African-American religious experience, Wright did not hold back. Declaring his truth as a practitioner of the "prophetic theology of the black church," he made it crystal clear what the brand of religion Barack Obama had absorbed in the pews at Trinity United Church of Christ was. Though his language was devoid of the explicitly racist invective on the infamous recordings, his message of blacks as perpetually oppressed by white America was unchanged.

"If I see God as male," he declared, "if I see God as white male, if I see God as superior, as God over us and not Immanuel, which means 'God with us', if I see God as mean, vengeful, authoritarian, sexist, or misogynist, then I see humans through that lens. My theological lens shapes my anthropological lens. And as a result, white males are superior; all others are inferior. And I order my society where I can worship God on Sunday morning, wearing a black clergy robe, and kill others on Sunday evening, wearing a white Klan robe. I can have laws which favor whites over blacks, in America or South Africa. I can construct a theology of apartheid, in the Afrikaner church, and a theology of white supremacy in the North American or Germanic church. The implications from the outset are obvious."

Wright continued...

"...To say, 'I am a Christian,' is not enough. Why? Because the Christianity of the slaveholder is not the Christianity of the slave. The God to whom the slaveholders pray, as they ride on the decks of the slave ship, is not the God to whom the enslaved are praying, as they ride beneath the decks on that same slave ship.

"How we are seeing God, our theology, is not the same. And what we both mean when we say, 'I am a Christian,' is not the same thing. The prophetic theology of the black church has always seen and still sees all of God's children as sisters and brothers, equals who need reconciliation, who need to be reconciled as equals in order for us to walk together into the future which God has prepared for us."

In brief, Wright was confirming that in his view, long propounded in the black church where Obama, for all his belated protestations, had been nurtured spiritually and politically, the God of white men is a racist god.

The questions that might have followed were clear:

Was Obama imbued with the same righteous racial indignation that Wright freely advertised? Was he bent on the same "liberation, transformation and reconciliation" Wright demanded as a necessary process for the redemption of America?

But the implications were left uncovered. As far as the vast majority of Americans were concerned, the pertinent questions had already been addressed in Obama's guileful and evasive speech.

And to the extent the problem still existed, the "More Perfect Union" speech provided the obvious and, for Obama, the natural path forward.

Lie.

Indeed, the day after Reverend Wright's appearance at the National Press Club, Obama doubled down in a speech in Hickory, North Carolina.

"I have spent my entire adult life trying to bridge the gap between different kinds of people," he proclaimed. "That's in my DNA, trying to promote mutual understanding to insist that we all share common hopes and common dreams as Americans and as human beings. That's who I am. That's what I believe. That's what this campaign has been about."

As for Reverend Wright, he'd been shocked, *shocked* by his words.

"Yesterday, we saw a very different vision of America. I am outraged by the comments that were made and saddened over the spectacle that we saw yesterday.

"You know, I have been a member of Trinity United Church of Christ since 1992. I have known Rev. Wright for almost 20 years. The person I saw yesterday was not the person that I met 20 years ago. His comments were not only divisive and destructive, but I believe that they end up giving comfort to those who prey on hate, and I believe that they do not portray accurately the perspective of the black church.

"They certainly don't portray accurately my values and beliefs. And, if Rev. Wright thinks that that's political posturing, as he put it, then he doesn't know me very well. And based on his remarks yesterday, well, I may not know him as well as I thought, either."

That was more than enough for a media that was already moving beyond generosity to outright worship.

Newsweek's Richard Wolffe, for example, made Obama out to be the victim.

"Many pundits have wondered aloud why Barack Obama has not had a Sister Souljah moment in this campaign, evoking Bill Clinton's 1992 repudiation of the hip-hop star's inflammatory and racist comments," Wolffe wrote. "In Winston-Salem Obama went far beyond Clinton's criticism, disowning his former pastor—and running the risk of alienating a community on the South Side of Chicago that has been among his most ardent supporters."

And then the white-knighting went into turbocharge.

"Yet it didn't sound as though Obama was in the mood for political calculation on Tuesday. Instead, he appeared dismayed not just by the offensive nature of Wright's comments—specifically Wright's accusations that the U.S. government had unleashed HIV/AIDS on the African-American community and engaged in 'terrorism' overseas. He also seemed offended by Wright's suggestion that his speech on race in Philadelphia was a case of political pandering."

Other legacy media coverage was similarly dismissive of the fact Wright had exposed everything Barack Obama had said in his famous Philadelphia speech on race as a lie.

And there was even less interest in examining the other, shall we say, *problematic* elements of Obama's past – for instance, the long and profitable association he'd had with Tony Rezko, a land baron and restaurant franchisee who contributed more than a quarter-million dollars to his campaigns.

But Rezko was standard issue political corruption, so familiar to be readily dismissed by both reporters and the general public. Looming far more ominously for America was the reality that, far from out of character, Obama's association with Wright was part of a lifelong pattern. In fact, his entire history was studded with close relationships with people on the most extreme edge of America's radical fringe.

Chief among these was Obama's long-standing and highly useful friendship with former (and wholly unrepentant) Weather Underground terrorist Bill Ayers. By his own admission, Obama and Ayers had such a close friendship that they had regularly babysat each others' children. Moreover, it was in Ayers' living room that Obama's political career had been launched with a 1995 campaign fundraiser. And Ayers almost certainly ghostwrote much if not all of *Dreams from My Father*, Obama's first memoir, which would be pivotal in establishing his national reputation and his brand.

He also had a deep personal relationship with a pair of Palestinian academics known for their radical and anti-Semitic views: Edward Said, under whom Obama had studied at Columbia, and Rashid Khalidi, a close Obama friend during his time at the University of Chicago, who then moved on to Columbia. With so many of the Obama campaign's key donors being prominent Jewish Americans, had they been publicized those connections might have been highly inconvenient. In Khalidi's case there was actually a video locked away in the archives of the *Los Angeles Times* of a going-away party for Khalidi as he left the University of Chicago for Columbia at which Obama spoke – reportedly releasing a fusillade of incendiary anti-Israeli rhetoric. But the *Times* refused to release the video, citing the wishes of its source. American voters would never know how chummy Obama was with Hamas-affiliated Palestinians.

Damaging, too – had it been widely known – would have been Obama's mentorship by Harvard and New York

University law professor Derrick Bell, one of the pioneers of Critical Race Theory, the noxious philosophy that defines America as "systemically racist" and which would come to quietly underlie Obama's policy agenda, eventually coming to full flower in the Black Lives Matter movement. The candidate's relationship with Bell was never so much as a footnote in the coverage of the 2008 campaign.

Hardly least, there was Frank Marshall Davis, the Stalinist writer and suspected Soviet intelligence asset who mentored Obama as a youngster in Hawaii.

But no questions were asked about that, either.

The door had to be shut on the public's understanding of those affiliations, because if mainstream America recognized the full extent of Barack Obama's radical associations and influences there was no way he could have closed the sale with the public. He wouldn't beat Hillary Clinton, and even if he somehow did, with all the un-American baggage trailing him, it would likely have made defeating war hero John McCain, the Republican nominee, an insurmountable task.

A compliant mainstream media let Obama off the hook and never challenged him for any of it, starting with his brush-off of the pastor he had used and discarded. Nor was any connection made between Wright's angry rhetoric from the pulpit and Obama's actions – both before becoming president and after.

Nothing more at all was made of Wright – not even by John McCain, who in a self destructive show of civility, refused to allow his campaign to run ads showing the reverend's incendiary American-hating sermons. But above all it was the mainstream media's dogged refusal to play tapes that showed the public what sort of people Obama had associate with throughout his adult life that was the most naked betrayal of the public trust. That willful covering up of the past was central to Obama's 2008 presidential campaign, and it would extend to the obfuscation of the whole of his background, influences and ideology.

Moreover, following his election, the media reflex to protect Obama at all costs – to turn away from ugly realities and ignore inconvenient facts – became the new normal. And by now, under the addled and corrupt Biden, it has virtually reached the level of farce.

Needless to say, truth-stretching had long come easily to politicians almost everywhere. But until recently those who aspired to high office in America understood, or learned the hard way, that there were lines that could not be crossed. Richard Nixon was forced to resign less for the Watergate break-in than for the cover-up, when it became clear to the American people they'd been lied to. George H.W. Bush's broken pledge of "No new taxes" cost him the Oval Office. While Bill Clinton beat the impeachment for his lies about sexual misconduct, in its aftermath both his personal stature and that of the presidency were irreparably diminished. And though it's an open question whether George W. Bush intentionally misled the public on Saddam Hussein's WMD (or, indeed, whether in the final analysis such conjecture was actually false), the left won the PR war with the 'Bush lied, people died' mantra.

Quite simply, there is a long American tradition of public outrage when we find out our government is lying to us.

Yet Barack Obama not only lied his way into office, he then lied his way through the next eight years. Indeed, the lies of Obama's two terms – and those of the former vice president (long a shameless, egregious small-time fraud) over whom Obama and his lieutenants continue to exercise full control – have been like nothing we've ever seen. Theirs have been lies of staggering audacity, lies about the very character of America and its people, its history and its traditions. They are lies that have cast the greatest nation in the history of the world as the world's greatest outpost of bigotry and oppression.

Moreover, they have enforced these outrageous lies through an unprecedented regime of calumny and censorship, brutally enforcing prohibitions on truth and even reality. To challenge any of it is to be a "conspiracy theorist" and banned from social media as purveying "disinformation"; worse, to be stripped of employment or find oneself under special scrutiny by government agents.

The lying has been conscienceless, but it has not been without purpose. "Morality is entirely subordinate to the interests of class war,' declared Lenin. "Everything is moral that is necessary for the annihilation of the old exploiting order and for uniting the proletariat." Exchange the archaic-sounding "proletariat" for "the credulous" or simply "Democrats," and it is the dictum Barack Obama has followed has entire public life.

The result is an America we no longer recognize. It is an America where the insanity that men are women and women are men is official dogma; where the public is placed under a medical regime with no regard for truth or science; where our great cities are cesspools of depravity and rampant crime goes unpunished; where our borders are no longer worthy of the term; where even a former president is subject to the Soviet butcher Lavrentiy Beria's rule of "Show me the man and I'll show you the crime."

And it is an America where we have turned on one another in ways unimaginable since the Civil War.

In the decades before Obama, America made astonishing progress on the racial front. Barriers that had stood for centuries had fallen, optimism for ethnic harmony was rampant. Obama's own election to the presidency was widely regarded as proof that the long-sought coming together of the races in America was at hand.

Instead, we live today in an America where race and ethnicity are exalted and individuality is regarded with disdain and where half the country – that half in control of our preeminent institutions – has fully embraced the lie that the other half are "white supremacists."

This is all the work of our 45th president, the great divider, Barack Hussein Obama. He pledged to "fundamentally transform" America.

That is the one thing he didn't lie about.

CHAPTER 3

RED DIAPER BABY

Over the years, there have been a number of revealing Obama biographies, though, in a media environment characterized by slavish devotion to the 42nd president, none has had nearly the impact it deserved. Chief among them, especially on the crucial subject of Obama's formative years, are Stanley Kurtz's *Radical-in-Chief: Barack Obama and the Untold Story of American Socialism*, Paul Kengor's *The Communist: Frank Marshall Davis: The Untold Story Of Barack Obama's Mentor* and David Garrow's *Rising Star*.

Obama's own memoir, *Dreams from My Father*, was almost certainly ghostwritten by Bill Ayers. And, of course, this is the Obama origin story that continues to be taken as gospel by most Americans.

In fact, in its most crucial respects, it is self serving fiction. As historian Garrow, a former Pulitzer Prize winner for his majestic biography of Martin Luther King, says of the start of his research on his own Obama book, "I read *Dreams* and thought, 'This is a crock.' It's not history. It's all make-believe."

He went on to unearth a variety of sources, including several of the women in the young Obama's life, (and his often revealing letters to them), that had gone ignored by the media; and which in sum present the picture of an ambitious, deeply unscrupulous and self absorbed young man, who even then was drawn to black racialism and anti-Americanism.

The focus in Obama's account is on his search for a connection with Barack Obama, Sr., a Kenyan student who is lionized in its pages. The future president depicts himself as struggling between the legacies of a Kenyan idealist father and a white American mother from Kansas, ultimately choosing the former, and enabling him to emerge as the wise and knowing figure he is today.

Following his election, the conservative pundit and (later) documentary filmmaker Dinesh D'Souza, drawing on his own personal experiences, wrote a book entitled *The Roots of Obama's Rage*, pegging the president as an anti-colonialist. For D'Souza, the experience of a Kenyan revolutionary throwing out British rule seemed identical ideologically to what he'd seen in his own native India, and it was key to defining who and what the younger Obama would become. There is clearly something to this. It is certainly a partial explanation for Obama's enduring hostility toward the West and its sustaining institutions.

But by now it is clear that anticolonialism was not Barack Obama's primary ideological motivation. Anti-Americanism and Marxism-Leninism were. He is an anti-American and a racist. His intention was never to heal us. It was to drive a wedge through our national heart and use the destruction to usher in an America unrecognizable 15 years later.

Dreams From My Father is often self-serving and inaccurate, especially in regard to his views of race. In Obama's account of his life, he split with one white girlfriend after she failed to show regard for black nationalist views presented in an August Wilson play. In fact, as biographer Garrow discovered, Obama's relationship with the girlfriend, Sheila Miyoshi Jager, ended after their visit to an exhibit on the trial of Nazi Holocaust architect Adolf Eichmann led to a heated argument over the charge by a Nation of Islam leader named Steve Cokely that Jewish doctors were injecting black babies with the AIDS virus in order to perpetrate a Holocaust against blacks. Jager was shocked to discover that Obama was so infatuated with black radical politics that he refused to condemn this or even deny that it was false.

But Obama's account was false not only in its details, but in its thrust. Barack Obama, Sr., supposedly his son's inspiration and model, was himself far from the idealistic young anti-colonialist portrayed in *Dreams From My Father*. Rather, he was a future corrupt bureaucrat and Nairobi politico who talked a good game while living a deplorable, abusive personal life. Nor, in fact, was he even necessarily the actual father of the future American president.

Of course, any suggestion Barack Obama isn't who he says he is immediately meets with ridicule from the media, and when the subject of Frank Marshall Davis belatedly inched into the edges of public consciousness, the Praetorian Guard of "fact-checkers" went into overdrive. The official version of the story was again trotted out for public consumption.

The account from *Dreams from My Father* has it that after meeting the senior Barack Obama in a Russian language class at the University of Hawaii in the fall of 1962, Ann and Barack Sr. were married in February of 1963, in advance of the birth of Barack, Jr. in August of the same year. But Barack, Sr., who already had a wife back home in Kenya, was soon in Cambridge, Massachusetts, attending graduate school at Harvard, and would not meet Barack, Jr. until the boy was 10 years old.

Ann Dunham, meanwhile, relocated with her infant son to Seattle for her sophomore year at the University of Washington. Subsequently, she remarried, moved to Indonesia and later deposited Barack with her parents in Honolulu.

As *Dreams From My Father* tells it, Davis also happened to be living in Honolulu, and Barack's grandfather Stanley Dunham periodically brought the boy around to Davis's home.

This tale is bizarre in a number of respects.

Of all the grownups to whom a child might be willingly exposed, few would have been less savory than Frank Marshall

Davis – unless, that is, there were reasons for fostering the relationship.

Documentary filmmaker Joel Gilbert engaged in two years of scrupulous research for his 2012 film, *Dreams From My Real Father*, along the way unearthing obscure film footage and photos. Among his finds were nude shots of Barack Obama's mother, Ann Dunham, which had been available via a mail-order catalog connected to Frank Marshall Davis. The old radical had been a photography bug going back to his days in Chicago, with a penchant for pornography and a particular taste for nudes of young white girls. Though hurriedly – and baselessly – challenged as disinformation by mainstream sources, they make plain that, at minimum, Davis knew young Ann Dunham at the time of her son's birth and that she had posed nude for him.

But Gilbert also uncovered Davis's autobiographical novel *Sex Rebel: Black*, which contained an account of a sexual relationship with a young white girl named "Anne."

And, surely, at the very least, Ann's parents knew of his lurid sexual hobbies; he had girls coming in and out of his house all the time.

While these elements do not conclusively establish a sexual relationship between young Ann Dunham and Frank Marshall Davis, the circumstantial evidence is compelling.

So, too, is the evidence of one's eyes. For, by anyone's reckoning, in side-by-side-by-side photographs of Davis and the future president, the resemblance is striking, while in the case of the elder Obama, it is almost non-existent.

Strong as the evidence is suggesting Davis is Obama's biological father, what matters more – and is far more meaningful – is that Frank Marshall Davis is Barack Obama's ideological and intellectual father.

Davis was a veteran communist, long on the FBI's watch list. There was a standing order that, should the U.S. become involved in an active war with the Soviet Union, he be indefinitely detained for national security purposes.

And for good reason. Here's the oath you took as a member of the Communist Party USA...

"I pledge myself to rally the masses to defend the Soviet Union, the land of victorious socialism. I pledge myself to remain at all times a vigilant and firm defender of the Leninist line of the Party, the only line that insures the triumph of Soviet Power in the United States."

In the print version of *Dreams From My Father*, originally published to limited attention in 1995, Davis is referred to 22 times. In the book he's simply called "Frank," and presented as a friend of Obama's grandfather who "lived in a dilapidated house in a run-down section of Waikiki."

Tellingly, "Frank" disappears from the audio version, produced after Obama's political career, and presidential ambitions, were underway.

The size of the role Davis played in the life of the future president has of course been ignored by the entire legacy corporate media.

Who was Frank Marshall Davis? Born in 1905 in Arkansas City, Kansas, south of Wichita, Davis attended both Friends University and Kansas State Agricultural College, now Kansas State University, but never graduated from college. Instead, he left for Chicago, and for the next several years wrote for black newspapers – the *Chicago Evening Bulletin*, the *Chicago Whip*, and the *Gary American* – before leaving in 1931 for Atlanta and landing an editing job for a black twice-weekly. Ultimately known as the *Atlanta Daily World*, it was America's most successful black daily.

Along the way, Davis compiled an archive of poetry, which by 1935 resulted in a book entitled *Black Man's Verse*. What was in it? From the Poetry Foundation comes a review…

"A critical success," Black Man's Verse "is experimental, cacophonous, yet sometimes harmonious…" The volume includes poems such as "Giles Johnson, Ph.D.," in which, despite his four college degrees and knowledge of Latin and Greek, the title character starves to death because he does not wish to do the manual labor that made up the majority of work available to blacks. Other pieces in Black Man's Verse —"Lynched," "Mojo Mike's Beer Garden," and "Cabaret"— make use of Davis's expertise on jazz to evoke "the spirit of protest in jazz and free verse with . . . objections to racial oppression, producing a poetry that loudly declaims against injustice." Another piece, entitled "Ebony Under Granite," discusses the lives of various black people buried in a cemetery, including a reverend who'd have sex with most of the women in his congregation, a two-dollar prostitute, and a man who'd served life in prison for voting more than once in Mississippi. Tellingly, there was also one Roosevelt Smith,

a black writer so frustrated by literary critics that he became a postman.

Having initially expressed some doubts about the Communist Party USA (CPUSA) and its leadership, by the mid-1930's Davis had joined a number of its various affiliated organizations and was a full-blown supporter.

At the time, the infamous Scottsboro case, involving nine young black men falsely accused of raping a pair of white women and convicted in a kangaroo court, was the American Communist Party's great *cause célèbre*, and, on orders from the Communist International in Moscow, played up for propaganda purposes at every opportunity.

But in an era when injustice against blacks was rampant, and largely overlooked by the mainstream parties, agitation on behalf of blacks was more than just a successful CPUSA recruiting tool. From the outset, the active promotion of racial strife and division was a key part of the communist plan to destroy the country itself.

In the Scottsboro case, the Party found an unprecedented opportunity. In the midst of the turmoil, behind the scenes they actually produced a strategy, in writing, outlining the overthrow of racist Southern state governments and the establishment of a separatist Black Communist republic.

The mainstream black civil rights leadership, led by the NAACP, wanted none of this, denouncing the communist attempt to hijack the case. But Davis was all in, as he was also on the Party's other great cause of the time, the case of black Atlanta communist agitator Angelo Herndon, convicted under Georgia's insurrection law for his attempts to create the CPUSA's Southern black separatist state.

In a 1950 FBI report unearthed by Paul Kengor, it was recorded that Davis initially "became interested in the Communist Party in 1931, while he was Editor of the *Atlanta Daily World*, a Negro newspaper. Subject stated he became interested in the Communist Party mainly because of the Scottsboro case and later because of the Herndon case."

Herndon was, in Davis' words, a "young black Communist" who, in "an act of unbelievable courage," had led a march on the Georgia state capitol.

In his editorials in the *Atlanta Daily World*, Davis promoted communist luminaries like the black poet Langston Hughes and the economic theorist J.B. Matthews, who later recanted communism and became the chief investigator for the House Un-American Activities Committee.

"It is a fact that the Negro, getting the dirty end of the economic, social and political stick, finds in Communistic ideals those panacea he seeks," he wrote in one editorial, and in another: "I believe that were our government adjusted according to Red standards, few members of the kaleidoscopic race would have sense enough to take advantage of it."

Nonetheless, by the mid-1930's, Davis was personally taking advantage of government largesse, catching federal Works Progress Administration grant money to write poetry; and in 1937, he received a coveted Julius Rosenwald Fellowship, endowed by the creator of the Sears Roebuck empire to advance black progress. Davis's career peaked when he became executive editor of the Associated Negro Press, a news service for black newspapers, holding the position until 1947, which made a boy born poor and disadvantaged a successful and prominent figure within his professional circle.

Indeed, like Obama himself, his future mentor might have had every reason to laud the social mobility uniquely available in America to those of all backgrounds, rather than focusing obsessively on the country's shortcomings.

But that was apparently beyond him. Marinated in grievance born of a series of ugly racial incidents in his youth, Davis found solutions not in the flawed but ever-evolving processes of the American system, but in the blunt brutality of Stalinism.

He became especially close to Paul Robeson, the internationally known black actor and singer, who was among the Soviets' chief American apologists. Davis frequently cited Robeson in his columns and in 1940 – when the Russians were still allied with Hitler, and opposed American entry into the war – he attended a CPUSA-sponsored "peace mobilization" conference headlined by Robeson. (Not incidentally, the conference was also attended by the noted communist agitator Richard Walker, whose granddaughter, Valerie Jarrett, would later serve as Barack Obama's closest advisor in the White House.)

As Davis would later explain in his memoir, he was driven, above all, "to join hands with others seriously interested in curing the disease of American racism. ...I knew I would be described as a Communist, but frankly I had reached the stage where I didn't give a damn…The genuine Communists I knew as well as others so labeled had one principle in common: to use any and every means to abolish racism. From now on, I would join hands with anybody going my way…My sole criterion was this: Are you with me in my determination to wipe out white supremacy?"

In Davis' view, capitalist America was an irredeemably racist hellhole while Stalin's USSR was a paradise of equality for all – this, even while Stalin's gulags were executing dissidents and other undesirables by the millions. The USSR was also a nation where each ethnic and religious group was required to carry an internal passport identifying themselves by their ethnicity and sect. In other words, it was based upon a system in which one's identity determined where you might go, whether or not you were employed and most of the other basic facts of everyday life. Ironically, Davis preferred this to what mainstream civil rights organizations favored: the elimination of legal segregation.

In the post-war years, Davis became a vitriolic critic of Winston Churchill, following the latter's denunciation of the Soviet-imposed "iron curtain" falling over Eastern Europe. In his columns for the Associated Negro Press, he excoriated Churchill for his promotion of the idea that an Anglo-American alliance should dominate the geopolitical scene, rather than more deserving nations like "Russia and China."

Fifty years later, Barack Obama would provoke a political row by summarily banishing Winston Churchill's bust from the Oval Office. It was widely assumed then that the move was prompted by Barack Obama Sr.'s, long-ago links to the Kenyan independence movement that Churchill had vigorously opposed. But this more likely reflects the influence of Frank Marshall Davis.

Indeed, after the war, Frank Marshall Davis's radicalism bloomed like a red tide. "As the victorious white army liberated various parts of Europe from the Axis," he wrote in his memoir, "they had begun to replace European fascism with 'the American way of life' and its tradition of racism."

He soon started a communist newspaper of his own, the *Chicago Star*, around the same time marrying fellow Communist Helen Canfield, a white woman 19 years his junior. She was 21.

Of the dozen or so communist-affiliated organizations in Chicago with which Davis was then associated – including the Civil Rights Congress, the Chicago Civil Liberties Committee and American Youth for Democracy – one, Citizens' Committee to Aid Packing-House Workers, is of particular note in terms of understanding the origins of the constellation of figures who would appear around Obama when he became a senator and President. Davis' ally in the Packing-House organization's publicity committee was one Vernon Jarrett, a leftist columnist for the *Chicago Tribune* and later the *Chicago Sun-Times*. His son, Dr. William Robert Jarrett, would marry Valerie Bowman – better known later as Valerie Jarrett. Thus, Frank Marshall Davis was on close terms with both grandfathers of Valerie Jarrett, who would herself wind up President Barack Obama's most trusted adviser.

From 1946 to 1948, the *Chicago Star* – sarcastically nicknamed the Red Star for its non-stop Stalinist propaganda – featured Frank Marshall Davis's opinion columns and those of other hard-core leftists, including Soviet agents like Johannes Steel, Howard Fast, and Lee Pressman. In his columns, Davis inveighed endlessly against "American imperialism," "Red-baiting," and "the big money boys and the high priests of rising American fascism."

His approach was not subtle. "The Ku Klux Klan is international," he screamed in a typical screed on August 24, 1946, "... The forces supporting racism and attacks on Negroes are the same forces seeking to wreck the new Poland, Yugoslavia and China and who want to get tough with Russia."

As Davis had it, while America's Congress was busy debating "phony" tax cuts that would "only help the rich," the Soviets were on the verge of curing cancer. On the religious front, Davis pushed the communist trope, (today a cornerstone of progressive church doctrine) that Jesus was essentially a socialist. "The evidence of logic and history should align the deeply religious with believers in socialism and communism," he wrote.

It is almost certain that by then Davis was a Soviet agent, the financing to keep his small-circulation newspaper in business coming from Moscow through a network of union cutouts. Other than Davis, the *Star*'s founders were one Bill Sennett, identified by the House Un-American Activities Committee as a "Chicago Communist Party organizer," Ernest DeMaio, a.k.a. Jack Conroy, a CPUSA organizer and president of an electrical workers' union, the known communist apparatchik William Patterson and Grant Oakes, another union organizer with ties to many identified communist front organizations. All of this came to light as a result of congressional and other official investigations of communist activities in the late 1940's and early 1950's, the information later confirmed when the Soviet KGB files were opened to public view following the fall of the USSR.

However, in 1948, the *Chicago Star* was sold and renamed the *Illinois Standard*, and Davis and his wife practically vanished from the Chicago political scene. They turned up next in Hawaii.

In his memoirs, Davis credited Paul Robeson as the primary influence behind his move to Honolulu in 1948. The previous year the singer had appeared there in a series of concerts sponsored by the International Longshoremen's and Warehousemen's Union (ILWU), the most powerful labor organization in the territory and, wrote Davis, "Paul enthusiastically supported our pending trip."

No sooner had Davis made his way to Hawaii and agreed to a full-time job as a columnist for the *Honolulu Record* than its editor, Koji Ariyoshi, and six others were identified as communists and convicted under the Smith Act for "conspiring to teach and advocate the overthrow of the government by force and violence."

Paul Kengor's research indicates that as far back as 1935 the Communist International (Comintern) had identified

Hawaii as an area of opportunity for Soviet expansion, and over the course of the next 20 years communist agitators were placed on the islands with jobs and sinecures in hopes of sowing a revolt that would make the islands an independent communist bastion in the Pacific.

This plan of placing red salts in paradise almost certainly included Davis.

However, Davis's racial agitation in Hawaii did not go well. Edward Berman, an official with the NAACP in Hawaii, wrote that "one Frank Marshall Davis, formerly of Chicago (and formerly editor of the Chicago Communist paper, the *Star*), suddenly appeared on the scene to propagandize the membership about our 'racial problems' in Hawaii. He had just sneaked in here on a boat, and presto, was an 'expert' on racial problems in Hawaii."

A liberal rather than an out-and-out leftist, Berman had been around and by then seen communists infiltrate and wreck liberal organizations in Hawaii. "There is no segregation here," he wrote NAACP head Roy Wilkins, Davis was angling to "create a mythical racial problem here." He added that the "influx of this element" – communist activism – had "frightened away ... scores of Negro (NAACP) members."

He told Wilkins he'd better have the guts to purge Frank Marshall Davis, "Otherwise you'll have a branch exclusively composed of yelping Stalinists and their dupes—characters who are more concerned about the speedy assassination of Tito [in Yugoslavia] than they are about the advancement of the colored people of these United States."

When the NAACP failed to greet him with open arms, Davis started the rival Hawaii Civil Liberties Congress, an analog for an organization he'd begun back in Chicago. A later congressional report said of this "ostensible civil-rights group," that it was "the most effective sounding board for communism in the Territory of Hawaii."

By May of 1949, Davis was back to writing anti-American screeds, now for the re-staffed *Honolulu Record*. Among other things, Davis trashed Truman over his decision to support an independent South Korea, demanding that America vacate the Korean peninsula and leave it to the tender mercies of Kim Il-Sung and the North Korean army. He offered similar sentiments about Vietnam, and the French colonials embroiled in conflict with the communist insurgency there.

But mostly Davis focused on race. "A nation which has white supremacy as its internal policy would obviously support white supremacy internationally," he wrote. "It is quite consistent for us to block the attempts of non-white peoples in the rest of the world to get freedom and equality."

He also consistently pushed the well-worn line that it was racists responsible for deriding him and others as communists, in retaliation for their civil rights activism. "I, personally, have no intention of letting the cry of 'communism' sidetrack me from my goal of complete civil rights as guaranteed by the Constitution," he wrote in one *Record* column. "The fight for absolute equality will continue. ... I want civil rights for all people."

At the time, Davis's self-characterization as a well-intentioned civil rights worker unjustly targeted by bigots both in and outside of government had little effect; his inflammatory politics had simply been too long on display. But, in fact, those protestations would be of great use later on, when his affiliation with Obama became a matter of interest. For sixty years, much of the public (and media), ignorant of Stalinism and conditioned to regard the Fifties blacklist as an unparalleled evil, was willing to accept the claim that even those clearly identified as committed communist agents had been victims of McCarthyism.

Nonetheless, black CPUSA membership never took off during the period Frank Marshall Davis was active on the political scene. Even in their heyday, the Communists were a fringe element in American politics, the party largely composed of scolds and ne'er-do-wells, along with idealistic young people who were willfully blind to well-documented reality. In time, though, they would take to calling themselves "progressives," and to working within to undermine and replace the more mainstream elements of the Democratic Party.

Some Obama partisans have argued that by the time Davis came into young Barack's life he was no longer an active communist, but the evidence for that is unclear at best. We do know that as late as 1956, he appeared before a U.S. Senate Subcommittee hearing on "the scope of Soviet activity in the United States," and the report that followed naming Davis as "an identified member of the Communist Party," and citing most every organization he'd ever worked for as a communist party front group.

Ultimately, the FBI had a six-hundred-page file on Frank Marshall Davis. In that file were a host of interesting items.

One of them had to do with his strange interest in the photography of Hawaii's shorelines. It noted that on September 17, 1949, an informant had seen Davis at Manners Beach "photographing large sections of the coastline with a camera containing a telescopic lens." The informant "stated that DAVIS spent much of his time in this activity. He said this was the third different occasion DAVIS had been observed photographing shorelines and beachfronts. Informant advised that it did not appear he was photographing any particular objects."

This might seem curious given that shoreline photography wasn't the reason that Davis was a photographic hobbyist. The source for that was his desire to photograph nude women. A more plausible explanation might be that he was doing what spies regularly do: he was getting paid to take pictures of potential landing grounds in case a Russian or Chinese army decided to storm those gorgeous beaches one day. In any case, not taking any chances, the FBI put him on the Security Index at this time, meaning that he was deemed potentially dangerous to national security, so he could be detained or arrested in the event of a national emergency.

Whether in fact Davis retained CP membership when he took Obama under his wing is ultimately inconsequential, since by the late Fifties, the Hawaii chapter of CPUSA had disbanded and gone underground.

Hence, it is likely that when he was interviewed by the FBI on the subject on August 2, 1963, and denied belonging to the Communist Party, he was telling the truth. For by then Davis was a registered Democrat.

What matters is that, no matter under what label, his politics never changed. Indeed, into the Sixties he was still working closely communist front organizations. Most notable is the American Committee for Protection of Foreign Born (ACPFB), essentially a law firm that existed to defend the Communist Party and its members. According to a 1944 congressional report on communist activities it "was founded by the Communist Party to defend foreign-born communists sent to America by Moscow to foment trouble." For example, Harry Bridges, the leader of the longshoremen's union who served as Davis's paymaster in Hawaii, was Australian, and Davis' would-be boss at the *Honolulu Record*, Ariyoshi, was Japanese.

Frank Marshall Davis was still very much involved in ACPFB when Stanley Dunham first brought his grandson to meet the old communist newspaperman.

In a 2007 speech at New York University commemorating the placement of the CPUSA's archive in an NYU library, Marxist journalist Gerald Horne described how Davis befriended the Dunhams, "a Euro-American family – that had migrated to Honolulu from Kansas, and a young woman from this family eventually had a child with a young student from Kenya East Africa who goes by the name of

Barack Obama, who, retracing the steps of Davis, eventually decamped to Chicago."

The connection between Davis and Obama, said Horne, was "a decisive influence in helping [Obama] to find his present identity as an African American, a people who have been the least anti-communist and the most left-leaning of any constituency in this nation."

To get some sense of why Obama was eager for a father figure in his life and why Davis became so important to him that he was mentioned 22 times in his memoirs, we need to go back to Obama's childhood. Two years after Obama, Sr. and Ann Dunham split up, she took up with Lolo Soetoro. Soetoro was a fellow student she met after returning to the University of Hawaii, and in 1965 Soetoro and Ann Dunham wed. (Note: there is actually no record of the marriage of Obama and Dunham, Sr., and nobody seems to remember a ceremony for that first marriage, or even a marriage license. Nor do there appear to be any pictures of the supposed event.) Soetoro moved his new family to Indonesia, where he'd gotten a job helping to map Western New Guinea for the government. But Lolo, who soon landed himself a better gig in governmental relations for Union Oil Company, surprised his radical wife by starting to sound a whole lot like a proud American – preaching to his stepson and daughter the virtues of hard work, earning money, and getting ahead in the world. As Ann had little use for that kind of talk, she sent little Barack back to Hawaii. He was then ten years old, and he had now been abandoned by both of his parents: his mother and his father. In Hawaii, he was to live with his left-wing grandparents. They, in turn, brought him around to the funky shantytown Waikiki "arts community" known as the Jungle. This was where their good friend Frank Marshall Davis lived. And for the next eight years that was his upbringing – afternoons and evenings here and there hanging around with Davis.

While Obama attended private schools, including at the ritzy Punahou Academy, he was a stoner and lackadaisical student, part of something called the "Choom Gang." But his real and lasting political and moral education appears to have been at the feet of Frank Marshall Davis.

What kind of influence did Frank Marshall Davis have on teenage Barack Obama?

A few years later, as a student at California's Occidental College, Obama would write almost nothing for publication, just two poems. But one was entitled 'Pop.'

Sitting in his seat, a seat broad and broken
In, sprinkled with ashes,
Pop switches channels, takes another
Shot of Seagrams, neat, and asks
What to do with me, a green young man
Who fails to consider the
Flim and flam of the world, since
Things have been easy for me;
I stare hard at his face, a stare

That deflects off his brow;
I'm sure he's unaware of his
Dark, watery eyes, that
Glance in different directions,
And his slow, unwelcome twitches,
Fail to pass.
I listen, nod,
Listen, open, till I cling to his pale,
Beige T-shirt, yelling,
Yelling in his ears, that hang
With heavy lobes, but he's still telling
His joke, so I ask why
He's so unhappy, to which he replies...
But I don't care anymore, cause
He took too damn long, and from
Under my seat, I pull out the
Mirror I've been saving; I'm laughing,
Laughing loud, the blood rushing from his face
To mine, as he grows small,
A spot in my brain, something
That may be squeezed out, like a
Watermelon seed between
Two fingers.
Pop takes another shot, neat,
Points out the same amber
Stain on his shorts that I've got on mine, and
Makes me smell his smell, coming
From me; he switches channels, recites an old poem

He wrote before his mother died,
Stands, shouts, and asks
For a hug, as I shrink, my
Arms barely reaching around
His thick, oily neck, and his broad back; 'cause
I see my face, framed within
Pop's black-framed glasses
And know he's laughing too.

The first mention of Davis in the published version of *Dreams From My Father* comes in Chapter 4:

"Away from my mother, away from my grandparents, I was engaged in a fitful interior struggle. I was trying to raise myself to be a black man in America, and beyond the given of my appearance, no one around me seemed to know exactly what that meant."

But "Gramps" would bring him to card games with men he knew, some of whom were black. One was "a poet named Frank who lived in a dilapidated house in a run-down section of Waikiki," who…

"…had enjoyed some modest notoriety once, was a contemporary of Richard Wright and Langston Hughes during his years in Chicago — Gramps once showed me some of his work anthologized in a book of black poetry. But by the time I met Frank he must have been pushing eighty, with a big, dewlapped face and an ill-kempt gray Afro that made him look like an old, shaggy-maned lion…

"...I was intrigued by old Frank, with his books and whiskey breath and the hint of hard-earned knowledge behind the hooded eyes. The visits to his house always left me feeling vaguely uncomfortable, though, as if I were witnessing some complicated, unspoken transaction between the two men, a transaction I couldn't fully understand."

Davis was by then divorced and well past the point where he would have been expected to care about some half-white kid one of his card-game buddies brought around. Yet he took a serious interest in Barack Obama.

Dreams tells of one episode, immediately following an incident in which Obama's grandmother, Madelyn Dunham, upset over having been accosted by an aggressive black panhandler on a bus, complained about the panhandler's race – the episode he would later use to such advantage in his self-serving 'More Perfect Union' speech.

"That night, I drove into Waikiki, past the bright-lit hotels and down toward the Ala-Wai Canal. It took me a while to recognize the house, with its wobbly porch and low-pitched roof. Inside, the light was on, and I could see Frank sitting in his overstuffed chair, a book of poetry in his lap, his reading glasses slipping down his nose. I sat in the car, watching him for a time, then finally got out and tapped on the door. The old man barely looked up as he rose to undo the latch."

Davis gave the underage Obama a glass of whiskey and "I told Frank some of what had happened. He nodded and poured us each a shot. 'Funny cat, your grandfather,' he said.

'You know we grew up maybe fifty miles apart?' I shook my head. 'We sure did. Both of us lived near Wichita. We didn't know each other, of course. I was long gone by the time he was old enough to remember anything. I might have seen some of his people, though. Might've passed 'em on the street. If I did, I would've had to step off the sidewalk to give 'em room. ...'"

Then this...

"Frank opened his eyes. 'What I'm trying to tell you is, your grandma's right to be scared. She's at least as right as Stanley is. She understands that black people have a reason to hate. That's just how it is. For your sake, I wish it were otherwise. But it's not. So you might as well get used to it.'

"Frank closed his eyes again. His breathing slowed until he seemed to be asleep. I thought about waking him, then decided against it and walked back to the car. The earth shook under my feet, ready to crack open at any moment. I stopped, trying to steady myself, and knew for the first time that I was utterly alone."

Probably the story is embellished for effect. But the account of Frank Marshall Davis's worldview and its impact on Barack Obama's rings absolutely true. The old man's angry, black-centered perspective, nurtured by a lifetime of grievance, was a powerful force, and in the confused, mixed-race child of a broken home, searching for an identity and someone to look up to, it found particularly fertile ground.

Obama later notes that not long after, as he was about to depart for college, the old man sat him down again: "Understand something, boy," he cautioned the unworldly 17-year old. "You're not going to college to get educated. You're going there to get trained. They'll train you to want what you don't need. They'll train you to manipulate words so they don't mean anything anymore. They'll train you to forget what it is that you already know. They'll train you so good, you'll start believing what they tell you about equal opportunity and the American way and all that shit."

Obama is at pains to let us know he followed his mentor's advice – he didn't believe that shit and never would. He notes that as a freshman at Occidental College that fall of 1979, "To avoid being mistaken for a sellout, I chose my friends carefully. The more politically active black students. The foreign students. The Chicanos. The Marxist professors and structural feminists and punk-rock performance poets."

Decades later, when Obama was in the Oval Office, a fellow former Occidental student named John Drew described an especially telling evening he'd spent over Christmas vacation, 1980, with the future president and his roommate, Pakistani student Mohammed Hasan Chandoo.

"Barack and Hasan showed up at the house in a BMW, and then we went to a restaurant together," recalled Drew. "We had a nice meal, and then we came back to the house and smoked cigarettes and drank and argued politics."

For the next several hours, they discussed Marxism.

"He was arguing a straightforward Marxist-Leninist class-struggle point of view, which anticipated that there would be a revolution of the working class, led by revolutionaries, who would overthrow the capitalist system and institute a new socialist government that would redistribute the wealth."

"The idea was basically that wealthy people were exploiting others," said Drew. "That this was the secret of their wealth, that they weren't paying others enough for their work, and they were using and taking advantage of other people. He was convinced that a revolution would take place, and it would be a good thing."

How much of Frank Marshall Davis stayed with Obama into adulthood? There's also this from *Dreams*, on the "dilemma that old Frank had posed to me the year I left Hawaii," likening the "survivor's guilt that I could expect to experience if I ever did try to make money and had to pass the throngs of young black men on the corner as I made my way to a downtown office" to the "tensions that certain children in Altgeld" – a notorious Chicago housing project – "might suffer if they took too much pleasure in doing their schoolwork."

It was, in his view, an either/or proposition: be black or be white. And the old man's pupil would see to it that the racial tribalism implicit in such a view would became our current reality.

Gone, with Barack Obama, would be the idea that America was moving inexorably toward the colorblind society envisioned by Dr. Martin Luther King, Jr. That ideal has been replaced by Frank Marshall Davis's conviction that "the American way of life, and all that shit" is a fraud, and that racial reconciliation in America is impossible, because we are an unforgivably, inevitably unjust nation.

CHAPTER 4

DREAMS FROM THE GUY WHO LIVES IN MY NEIGHBORHOOD

T here is no better source for the proposition that Obama is, and has long been, a committed Marxist than *Radical-In-Chief: Barack Obama and the Untold Story of American Socialism* by Stanley Kurtz, formerly of Harvard and the University of Chicago. Kurtz began researching Obama's shadowy political origins during his initial run for the presidency, and what he unearthed, had it been about anyone else, would have sent alarm bells clanging in even the most liberal newsrooms.

As it was, the self-serving *Dreams From My Father* was allowed to stand as the unquestioned account of Obama's political evolution by a generation of journalists ready to trade its collective soul to mainstream – and put into the White House – the black "Hope and Change" progressive.

Yet, even so little as a serious examination of the origins of *Dreams From My Father* itself would have opened a pandora's box of troubles for Obama. For it would have become widely known that the book's ghost writer was almost assuredly William Charles Ayers.

Ayers, now approaching eighty, even today describes himself as a "radical, leftist, small-'c'communist," but that is selling himself way too short. What he was a top leader of the hyper-violent Weather Underground, avowed Marxists who from the late Sixties into the mid-Seventies sought the overthrow of America and its racist, capitalist system through a systematic campaign of terror bombings. "Our intention is to disrupt the empire..." read the group's damning manifesto *Prairie Fire*, "to incapacitate it, to put pressure on the cracks."

All told, the Weather Underground is held responsible for hundreds of bombings, claiming credit for, among others, attacks on the U.S. Capitol, the Pentagon, the State Department and innumerable corporate and financial institutions. It also engaged in deadly bank robberies and an assortment of other crimes.

Yet almost as sickening was their philosophical posturing, including the public assertion that all white babies are "tainted with the original sin of '[white] skin privilege'" and "all white babies are pigs." Ayers' wife and fellow terrorist Bernadine Dohrn was an open admirer of mass murderer Charles Manson, asserting he was one of the few who understood the evil of white America. In tribute to Manson, the Ayers/Dohrn cell used a four-fingered salute representing the fork used to stab the pregnant Sharon Tate.

In short, these were, and are, vile and evil people, the dregs of humanity.

In 1980, with Jimmy Carter in office, Ayers, Dohrn and other members of their cell turned themselves in, anticipating leniency; and, indeed, while she did a mere seven months, Ayers incredibly got off on a technicality. "Guilty as sin, free as a bird – what a country, America!" he exulted in his memoir, *Fugitive Days*. Many noted the irony that it was published on September 11, 2001.

Both Ayers and Dohrn came from privilege. Ayers' father was the CEO of Chicago power company Commonwealth Edison and Dohrn's father was a prominent Manhattan attorney. Returning to Chicago as retired terrorists, they remade themselves into *legal* hard left activists, busily undermining the system from within, Dohrn as a law professor, Ayers as Distinguished Professor of Education and Senior University Scholar at the University of Illinois at Chicago. Incredibly, in this role, over the decades he has been one of the nation's leading educational "reformers," spearheading the charge for "diversity" and "equity" at the expense of academic standards.

The couple lived comfortably in the city's ultra-progressive Hyde Park section, where among their friends and neighbors were Barack and Michelle Obama.

When this came to light during the campaign, Obama blithely dismissed his association with Ayers as casual at best. Ayers was just "a guy who lives in my neighborhood," he claimed, "not somebody who I exchange ideas with on a regular basis."

But it's clear the relationship went a lot deeper and that, among other things, *Dreams From My Father* was a collaboration. Ayers clearly did more than serve as a sympathetic sounding board. In fact, the evidence that Ayers wrote Obama's book is both circumstantial and overwhelming.

In 1990, the little-known Obama, at the time still in law school, received an advance of $125,000 from Simon & Schuster to write a memoir. The deal was negotiated by literary agent Jane Dystel, who contacted Obama after reading a *New York Times* profile prompted by his election as Harvard's first black law review president.

But Obama was not a writer, and had never evidenced any gift in that direction. In fact, aside from the couple of poems he wrote at Occidental, it appears the only thing he'd had published was a stilted and overwrought article in the Columbia University magazine *Sundial* titled "Breaking The War Mentality."

And for five years, he delivered nothing to his publisher. Zilch. Zero. Bupkis.

When the publisher dumped the contract, the enterprising Dystel got him another advance, this time from Times Books for $40,000 on the promise of delivery of the manuscript within a year. And then, suddenly, a book appeared – one remarkably similar in style, and even content, to the future memoir by his Chicago friend and neighbor, William Ayers.

Ayers is a natural writer, and a close analysis by conservative writer Jack Cashill makes evident the striking similarities in style and word usage. Where Obama's prose had hitherto shown itself to be dense and labored, Ayers wrote – and *Dreams* was written – with the natural grace of a professional.

Moreover, in construction *Dreams* is a near double for *Fugitive Days*, and the two memoirs even use many of the same metaphors.

Comparing the books forensically, Cashill found:

- According to the Flesch Reading Ease Score (FRES), *Fugitive Days* scores a 54 on reading ease and a 12th grade reading level and *Dreams* scores a 54.8 on reading ease and a 12th grade reading level, a near-exact match.
- Under the rubric "cusum analysis" or QSUM, *Fugitive Days* averaged 23.13 words a sentence and *Dreams* averaged 23.36 words a sentence.

Furthermore, notes Cashill, the QSUM score for *Audacity of Hope*, Obama's second book, would be strikingly different, averaging more than six extra words per sentence and clocking in at a 9th grade reading level. Clearly, the two Obama autobiographies were not written by the same hand.

But just as striking are the similarities of subject – and point of view. Both books offer a fierce critique of middle-class white American culture and are driven by an obsession with race.

"'I also thought I was black,' writes Ayers only half-jokingly, of his embarrassment at having been born white and to wealth and privilege. Establishing their racial *bona fides*, Ayers and Dohrn had named their first son "Malik" after the newly Islamic Malcolm X and their second "Zayd" after Zayd Shakur, a Black Panther killed in a shootout that claimed the life of a New Jersey State Trooper.

"Tellingly," writes Cashill, "Ayers, like Obama, began his career as a self-described 'community organizer,' Ayers in inner-city Cleveland, Obama in inner-city Chicago. In short, Ayers was fully capable of crawling inside Obama's head and relating in superior prose what the *Dreams'* author calls a 'rage at the white world [that] needed no object.'

"Indeed, in *Dreams*, it is on the subject of black rage that Obama writes most eloquently. Phrases like 'full of inarticulate resentments,' 'unruly maleness,' 'unadorned insistence on respect' and 'withdrawal into a smaller and smaller coil of rage' lace the book.

"In *Fugitive Days*, 'rage' rules and in high style as well. Ayers tells of how his 'rage got started' and how it evolved into an 'uncontrollable rage – fierce frenzy of fire and lava.'

Indeed, the Weathermen's inaugural act of mass violence was the 'Days of Rage' in 1969 Chicago.

"As in Chicago, that rage led Ayers to a sentiment with which Obama was altogether familiar, 'audacity!' Ayers writes, 'I felt the warrior rising up inside of me – audacity and courage, righteousness, of course, and more audacity.' This is one of several references.

"The combination of audacity and rage has produced two memoirs that follow oddly similar rules. Ayers describes his as 'a memory book,' one that deliberately blurs facts and changes identities and makes no claims at history. Obama says much the same. In *Dreams*, some characters are composites. Some appear out of precise chronology. Names have been changed."

"Obama's memoir was published in June 1995. Earlier that year, Ayers helped Obama, then a junior lawyer at a minor law firm, get appointed chairman of the multi-million-dollar Chicago Annenberg Challenge grant. In the fall of that same year, 1995, Ayers and his wife, Weatherwoman Bernardine Dohrn, helped blaze Obama's path to political power with a fundraiser in their Chicago home.

"In short," Cashill sums up, "Ayers had the means, the motive, the time, the place and the literary ability to jumpstart Obama's career. And, as Ayers had to know, a lovely memoir under Obama's belt made for a much better resume than an unfulfilled contract over his head."

When Kurtz, among others, pointed out that, contrary to Obama's denials, it was evident the two men were both friends and close political allies, the media had a meltdown, declaring the mounting evidence meaningless. "'McCarthyism' and 'Swiftboating' have come together in a particularly lethal and despicable form …" as the progressive legal scholar Stanley Fish termed it in the pages of the *New York Times*, noting that there was nothing remiss in Obama socializing with Ayers, since he "served with him on a board..."

On the face of it, it was an astonishingly brazen narrative. Ayers had never apologized for his past. To the contrary, on the publication of *Fugitive Days* he told the *New York Times* "I don't regret setting bombs...I feel we didn't do enough."

Is it possible to even guess at the outrage that would have ensued had it come to light that some Republican presidential hopeful had launched his political career at the home of, say, David Duke?

Nor was the board on which the two served as innocuous as pretended by progressive apologists. Founded by Ayers, it was called the Chicago Annenberg Challenge, and its explicit aim was the mass reshaping of young American minds.

Obama served on the CAC board until 2001, working closely with Ayers. As Kurtz observes, "CAC translated Mr. Ayers's radicalism into practice. Instead of funding schools directly, it required schools to affiliate with 'external partners,' which actually got the money. Proposals from groups focused on math/science achievement were turned down. Instead, CAC disbursed money through various far-left community organizers, such as the Association of Community Organizations for Reform Now (or ACORN)."

Barack Obama had, of course, spent time as an ACORN organizer.

The ex-Weatherman's rebirth as an educational reformer had been remarkably swift, his family's extensive cash and connections helping him burrow into the progressive elite community and push those views into policy.

But while going respectable obviously represented a change in tactics, Ayers' goals were unchanged. His aim was to use public education to bring about radical social change; i.e., to use the classroom as a vehicle for leftist indoctrination.

Remote as such a takeover once would have seemed, it was *the* key element in what is today recognized as the left's successful "long march through the institutions." With his talents, and with his immense drive and unyielding commitment to the cause, "that guy from the neighborhood" has been arguably the single greatest force in making it happen.

Little wonder that the Obama years would be particularly fruitful ones for Ayers. So active was he in formulating education policy under Obama that trying to run down all the threads connecting the Chicago Annenberg Challenge to federal education policy post-2008 is an endless crawl through rabbit holes.

Ayers was a leading advocate for Race to the Top, the multi-billion dollar U.S. Department of Education competitive grant program to support education "reform" and "innovation" in state and local district K-12 education, which has proven disastrous for educational performance in this country.

At the same time, Ayers pressed the Obama administration to downplay standardized testing in public schools,
maintaining that greater emphasis be placed on "collaborative
conversations" in classrooms, wherein the kids are given lots
of space to engage with teachers. Talk to those public-school
teachers who try to teach by that method, and most will say
"collaborative conversation" is a disaster. But for Ayers it's
part of the larger project of creating "diversity" and "social
justice" in schools.

Especially when it's black kids wanting to have "collaborative conversations" with white teachers about things like
how math is racist.

Indeed, Ayers has written extensively about the necessity
for "equity" in American education, from school funding, to
curriculum, to the necessity of always taking a child's race
and ethnicity into account. These ideas show up in particular in Race To The Top's focus on throwing money at bad
schools – specifically the $4 billion blown on "implement-
ing the bold reforms needed to transform the 5,000 lowest-
performing schools in America."

Ayers was also close with Obama Secretary of Commerce
Penny Pritzker, heiress to the Hyatt hotel chain fortune, with
whom he'd earlier served on the board of the Chicago Public
Education Fund, or just The Fund for short. One of The
Fund's projects was something called the GROW Network,
one of whose two founders, Ayers protégé Jason Zimba, is
credited by NPR as the "man behind" Common Core math.

The Pritzker family has also lavishly funded attempts to normalize transgenderism among children.

At the height of the 2008 campaign, when Kurtz sought to publicize the CAC records establishing both the depth of the Obama/Ayers bond, and their common goals, he was shut down. When, for instance, he arranged for a radio appearance on WGN, the Chicago talk station, to discuss his findings, the Obama campaign was invited to send a representative to present its side.

What happened instead would become familiar.

"It launched an all-out offensive against WGN," writes Herb Denenberg of Philadelphia's *Evening Bulletin*. "In an e-mail to supporters, the Obama campaign called Mr. Kurtz a 'slimy character assassin' whose 'divisive, destructive ranting' should be confronted." Next, an "unprecedented" barrage of e-mails and calls came to WGN protesting Kurtz's appearance. And obviously the campaign wouldn't send anyone to debate Kurtz.

What they tried to do instead, a decade before the term came into vogue, was cancel him.

Along the same lines, the campaign demanded that the U.S. Department of Justice prosecute a 501-c4 non-profit organization called the American Issues Project for running an advertisement on the ties between Obama and Ayers on the basis that it was engaging in campaign advocacy out of its bounds.

At the same time, the media was assiduously whitewashing candidate Obama's unsavory past. The influential *Wash-*

ington Post columnist Dana Milbank, for instance, scoffed at the idea Obama had been mentored in high school by a "member of the Soviet-controlled Communist Party," as well as at the notion Obama's political career began "in the home of a terrorist and killer" though both were not only true, but readily verifiable statements of fact.

Ultimately, those tactics worked. The media's suppression of Barack Obama's deeply troubling relationship with Bill Ayers was as tragically effective as all the rest, with devastating consequences. Firmly in place was a new method of lying from the top – when possible, by omission; and when not, because the facts were too apparent, with sneering and dismissive contempt.

CHAPTER 5

ORGANIZING FOR AMERICAN RUIN

"In 1983, I decided to become a community organizer," Barack Obama (and/or Ayers) writes in *Dreams From My Father.* "Now, with the benefit of hindsight, I can construct a certain logic to my decision, show how becoming an organizer was a part of that larger narrative, starting with my father and his father before him, my mother and her parents, my memories of Indonesia with its beggars and farmers and the loss of Lolo to power, on through Ray and Frank, Marcus and Regina; my move to New York; my father's death. I can see that my choices were never truly mine alone—and that that is how it should be, that to assert otherwise is to chase after a sorry sort of freedom."

Later, campaigning in Iowa early in his campaign for president, *The New York Times* would quote him as calling his community organizing experience "the best education I ever had, better than anything I got at Harvard Law School," and an education that was "seared into my brain."

Needless to say, The *Times* piece was deeply admiring, reflecting the view, as the candidate himself was at to pains to suggest, that the role and the "social justice" work it entails are unassailable: that they reflect a selflessness, a spirit of altruistic concern for the underdog and a fierce determination to right profound wrongs that represents mankind at its best.

No question it poll-tested well.

But what exactly *is* a community organizer?

What did it mean in practice, day to day? What did Obama actually *do* in his three years as a "grass roots organizer" on Chicago's impoverished South Side?

That crucial period of his life, too, prompted little mainstream curiosity; and, again, his own self-serving account was unchallenged by the legacy media. In fact, it was only after he'd secured the Democrat presidential nomination that the subject received widespread attention – and, then, only thanks to GOP vice presidential nominee Sarah Palin. Having been mocked by Democrats as an inexperienced former small-town mayor, Palin hit back with "I guess a small-town mayor is sort of like a community organizer, except that you have actual responsibilities."

The single reporter who had seriously investigated the subject before then was the *National Review's* Byron York, who spent time in Chicago and came back with a straight-forward report.

"Community organizing is most identified with the left-wing Chicago activist Saul Alinsky (1909-72), who pretty much defined the profession," he wrote. "In his classic book, *Rules for Radicals,* Alinsky wrote that a successful organizer should be 'an abrasive agent to rub raw the resentments of the people of the community; to fan latent hostilities of many of the people to the point of overt expressions.' Once such hostilities were 'whipped up to a fighting pitch,' Alinsky continued, the organizer steered his group toward confrontation, in the form of picketing, demonstrating, and general hell-raising."

"Perhaps the simplest way to describe community organizing," he noted further along, "is to say it is the practice of identifying a specific aggrieved population, say unemployed steelworkers, or itinerant fruit-pickers, or residents of a particularly bad neighborhood, and agitating them until they become so upset about their condition that they take collective action to put pressure on local, state, or federal officials to fix the problem, often by giving the affected group money. Organizers like to call that 'direct action'."

York says that the young Obama had a particular gift for the role, his intelligence and cool detachment enabling him to effectively bond disparate individuals into a cohesive unit, with a fixed purpose – as, indeed, would also be the case later.

As the director of something called the Developing Communities Project, Obama's community organizing goal was straightforward: to prompt government action (and increase government largesse) in a neighborhood marked by joblessness, fatherlessness, crime and every other kind of modern social dysfunction. In particular, he pressured Chicago's highly politicized city hall to install social welfare offices in the neighborhood, notably in the sprawling, crime-ridden public housing projects (like Altgeld Gardens, which he'd go on to cite in *Dreams*), organizing demonstrations to dramatize the demand.

"Obama got the ministers involved in several projects, without great success," writes York. "There was a push to get more city money for South Side parks after the Justice Department told the Chicago Park District it had to spend more on minority neighborhoods. There were plans for after-school programs, and job retraining for adults..."

Though he occasionally met with limited success, York adds crucially, "Obama's time in Chicago also revealed the conventionality of his approach to the underlying problems of the South Side. Is the area crippled by a culture of dysfunction? Demand summer jobs. Push for an after-school program. Convince the city to spend more on this or that. It was the same old stuff; Obama could think outside the box on ways to organize people, but not on what he was organizing them *for*.

"Certainly no one should live in an apartment contaminated by asbestos, but Obama did not seem to question, or at least question very strongly, the notion that the people he wanted to organize should be living in Altgeld at all. The place was, after all, one of the nation's capitals of dysfunction. 'Every ten years I would work on the census,' (local resident) Yvonne Lloyd told me. 'I always had Altgeld. When you look at those forms from the census, you had three or four generations in one apartment – the grandmother, the mother, the daughter, and then her baby. It was supposed to be a stepping-stone, but you've got people that are never going to leave'…Obama applied his considerable organizational skills to perpetuating the old, failed way of doing things."

In that sense, the future president was utterly and completely bound – bound so completely it was stronger than the daily evidence before his eyes – to that most fundamental tenet of leftist thought: that all problems of poverty, and want, and even criminality are the fault of the larger society, rather than a matter of personal responsibility; and that the solution was to be found in the state using its untrammeled power to level the playing field.

That oft-discredited idea had found renewed acceptance in the Sixties, taking such full hold within the Democratic Party that it soon became all but impossible for anyone in its ranks to stand up for the old verities of hard work and individual responsibility. This became all too apparent in 1965, when future Senator Daniel Patrick Moynihan, at the time a Harvard academic serving as assistant Secretary of Labor under Lyndon Johnson, issued his famous report warning of "the unraveling of the black family."

LBJ's massive War on Poverty had just been launched to address the gap between blacks and whites in income and other metrics of achievement and social mobility; the president and other liberals convinced, as ever, that if you threw enough money at a problem, you'd find the solution.

A clear and honest thinker – there were still a few Democrats like that back then – Moynihan dared to place the blame not on want of funding or "systemic racism" but where it belonged: on the choices and actions of the individuals involved. Describing the "tangle of pathologies" afflicting so many in the black inner cities, he stressed that "the heart of the deterioration of the fabric of Negro society is the deterioration of the Negro family," driven most notably by the absence of fathers in the home. "It is the fundamental source of the Negro community at the present time," he declared.

"More than most social scientists," as Kay Hymowitz later pointed out in *City Journal*, "Moynihan, steeped in history and anthropology, understood what families do. They 'shape their children's character and ability,' he wrote. 'By and large, adult conduct in society is learned as a child.' What children learned in the 'disorganized home[s]' of the ghetto, as he described through his forest of graphs, was that adults do not finish school, get jobs, or, in the case of men, take care of their children or obey the law. Marriage, on the other hand, provides a 'stable home' for children to learn common virtues."

In short, Moynihan posited that the problem might not be too little government, but too much. For absent reliable partners, single black mothers were increasingly reliant on welfare, resulting in a never-ending cycle of dependency.

The report was a beacon in the night – or should have been. It is worth noting that when it was written, in 1965, black illegitimacy stood at 24 percent; today, fully three quarters of black children grow up in homes without fathers.

Yet instead of the honest and difficult but much needed conversation it deserved, the report prompted outrage on the part of Democrats and civil rights leaders. Congress of Racial Equality (CORE) director Floyd McKissick summed up the left/liberal response to Moynihan's report, flatly asserting what would henceforth be the progressive mantra: "It's the damn system that needs changing." "Family instability is a 'peripheral issue,' echoed Whitney Young, executive director of the National Urban League. "The problem is discrimination."

Accused of outright bigotry, Moynihan dropped the subject, never meaningfully raising it again. Meanwhile, rather than making sustained efforts to reverse the pathologies and the underlying family/cultural deficit which produced them, the collectivist crowd redoubled its advocacy for America as an immutably terrible place.

This was emphatically Obama's view as he worked as a community organizer. Indeed, in the case of the future president, himself raised first by a single mother and then abandoned by her as well and raised by his grandmother, the contempt for Moynihan's stress on personal responsibility was also surely personal. Studies have it that that children from broken homes tend to lean harder left politically than those from intact families, and within the black community, to which in his post-college days Barack Obama was wedding himself passionately, the underclass is the greatest source of Democrat political strength.

It is not for nothing that in the years to follow, while making himself a major political figure in the party and then the nation, Obama would not speak of individual responsibility, but repeatedly of "collective salvation." He is nothing if not a talented speaker – it is his outstanding skill – and on no subject does he wax more passionately.

"They will tell you that the Americans who sleep in the streets and beg for food got there because they're all lazy or weak of spirit," he derides those who abide by the old virtues. "That the inner-city children who are trapped in dilapidated schools can't learn and won't learn and so we should just give up on them entirely. That the innocent people being slaughtered and expelled from their homes half a world away are somebody else's problem to take care of.

"I hope you don't listen to this. I hope you choose to broaden, and not contract, your ambit of concern. Not because you have an obligation to those who are less fortunate, although you do have that obligation. Not because you have a debt to all of those who helped you get to where you are, although you do have that debt.

"It's because you have an obligation to yourself. Because our individual salvation depends on collective salvation. And because it's only when you hitch your wagon to something larger than yourself that you will realize your true potential - and become full-grown."

It was a seductive pitch, to the young and the criminally naïve, and no one sells it better. As Stanley Kurtz observes, from the outset Obama's ideological program was "designed to ensnare the country in a new socialism, a stealth socialism that masquerades as a traditional American sense of fair play...."

To buy into this notion that poverty and despair are the result not of bad habits or behavioral pathologies – which might be remedied by lifestyle choices – but are the inevitable products of an unjust, racist capitalist society, is also to believe the lie that such misery can only be ameliorated by a redistributive and corrective government.

That this was a tragic delusion should have been apparent half a century ago, with the utter failure of the War On Poverty, and black neighborhoods going up in flames in the years that followed.

Had he been of a different mindset, or open-minded at all, this should have been obvious to Obama during his days as a community organizer.

The truisms of Moynihan's study haven't changed since the 1960's. We know even more definitively today that the formula for success in America is to get married before having children, graduate high school, avoid jail and hold at least an entry-level job. It is everywhere attainable, and it works.

The clearest evidence that it works is that immigrants unhandicapped by the culture of the inner city on average do better than Americans of any race. This emphatically includes immigrant Nigerians, who come from the same West African stock as do the vast majority of black Americans, and who, hardly coincidentally, are far more likely to vote Republican than American-born blacks. They're also far more likely to get and stay married, and they have average incomes above that of white Americans. Moreover, just twelve percent of black children living in two-parent homes are being raised in poverty. Plainly, discrimination isn't the problem. Family dysfunction, encouraged by welfare, is.

Progressive activists of the Obama stripe well know the statistics, and know too that stable two-parent families remain the greatest bulwark against collectivism. It is the reason for their ever more intense attacks on children, family, parental rights, including Democrat-allied teachers unions pushing for transgenderism and socialism.

On Obama's watch, the dysfunction Moynihan described accelerated at breakneck speed, leading to the moral dystopia of the present, where even titans of business must pay at least lip service to the virtues of the collectivist model.

For Barack Obama, the lifelong community organizer, the move from socialist revolutionary to "progressive" politician would be hardly any change at all, for the embrace of collectivism and contempt for individual choice and effort was the philosophy with which he'd come of age.

But for America, entrusting the future to such a man was a disaster.

CHAPTER 6

RIDIN' DIRTY

By every reasonable standard, Jack Ryan was the sort of man whose presence in the U.S. Senate would have been to the nation's benefit. Smart, attractive, well-spoken, with a highly appealing back story, even running as a Republican in Illinois, in 2004 Ryan was a formidable candidate,

But the public never got a chance to vote for Jack Ryan. After getting the GOP nomination, he was forced out of the race.

Barack Obama saw to that.

It was another crucial way in which it might be said he was ahead of his time. He was anticipating, as *The New Criterion's* James Bowman observed, "today's Democrats, who are working with a single purpose to maximize the opportunity for unfairness, if not fraud, in our elections."

Ryan had been a partner at Goldman Sachs, making hundreds of millions of dollars as an investment banker in both the firm's New York and Chicago offices. But in 2000, Ryan left Goldman Sachs, and started teaching at Hales Franciscan High School, an all-black institution where the vast majority of students came from poor families. For the four years he taught there, every one of the young men in the graduating classes went on to college.

That is to say, Jack Ryan had personally helped achieve exactly the thing Barack Obama and his community organizer pals held wasn't possible – an escape from poverty through hard work and individual achievement.

A Ryan-Obama clash would have been a referendum on the competing approaches. It might also have changed American history.

So what happened?

Ryan had formerly been married to Jeri Ryan, an actress who has appeared in, among other things, *Star Trek: Voyager*. They'd divorced five years before, in 1999, and the split had been ugly, as such things often are. The couple battled over custody of their five-year old son. Allegations were made. Jack accused Jeri of having an affair. She alleged that he'd pressured her to go with him to sex clubs, and this was why she'd fallen in love with another man.

It was seamy and unpleasant stuff, and in the interest of protecting the child, the divorce records were sealed.

On the positive side, the ugliness of the situation seems to have been what had driven Ryan to so radically alter his life's course.

And now, early in the Senate campaign, polls had him the overwhelming favorite to win the seat. Even Jeri Ryan supported his candidacy.

Yet almost as soon as Barack Obama became the Democrat nominee, rumors about what was in those sealed divorce records began to surface. Ryan had already released his tax records, but now the liberal *Chicago Tribune*, which had been the employer of Obama's political guru David Axelrod, dispatched its lawyers to get the divorce records unsealed.

Both Jack and Jeri asked that those stay sealed to protect their son.

Nonetheless, a Los Angeles judge named Robert Schnider unsealed the papers of the Ryans' divorce proceedings, setting off a media frenzy, and four days later Ryan dropped out of the race.

In retrospect, as one of the most gratuitous "sex scandals" in American history unfolded, no attention at all was paid to the genuine scandal that private divorce records had been unsealed for explicitly political purposes.

In an interview after his withdrawal, Ryan said he'd been flabbergasted by Schnider's decision, noting his lawyers had assured him there was "little chance of that happening and then we had to also think that some media organization would want to do that, which is the first time in the history of our country that someone said over the hopes and wishes of the mom and dad, release these documents to the world for everyone to see.

"We always thought we were going to win at the end and the judge suddenly flipped at the last minute and said the public right to know exceeds the health of the child and the judge found that the child would be harmed by the release of these documents. As any parent would know, you don't want disagreements between mom and dad put in front of the children. That's kind of parenting 101, I think."

No matter. The result, as intended, was the GOP was left without a candidate. The last-minute replacement was outspoken black conservative firebrand Alan Keyes, who not only had no base of support, but wasn't even an Illinois resident.

Thus, what would almost surely have been a decisive loss for Barack Obama was magically transformed into a springboard toward a limitless future. As the presumptive about-to-be senator, he went on to deliver his famous keynote at that year's Democratic convention and then to crush Keyes in November.

And before finishing his first Senate term, he would launch his presidential bid.

Even more telling about the vanishing candidacy of Jack Ryan: it was the *second* time in that 2004 race that such a mishap had befallen a formidable Obama opponent. Three months earlier, he had been trailing businessman/philanthropist Blair Hull by ten points in the race for the Democratic nomination, and Blair appeared unstoppable. "...As a former high school teacher, union worker, and board member of NARAL [the National Abortion Rights Action League], as *The Atlantic* summed it up, he "appeals to important Democratic constituencies; as the lone veteran in the field, he can oppose the war in Iraq unquestioned. His unusual life story, too, sets Hull apart from the drab lawyers, state representatives, and political scions who normally pursue office in Illinois."

Indeed, Hull's back story outshone even Obama's. A math genius, he'd developed a system for beating casinos at blackjack, translating it to quantitative analysis in stocks and making a huge fortune. That had enabled him to engage in large-scale giving to social justice causes.

But Axelrod's pals at the *Chicago Tribune* did Hull in also, this time leaking the claim that his second ex-wife, Brenda Sexton, had sought an order of protection against him during *their* 1998 divorce proceedings.

Again, those records were under seal, but again it didn't matter. The *New York Times* reported that "The *Tribune* reporter who wrote the original piece later acknowledged in print that the Obama camp had 'worked aggressively behind the scenes' to push the story," and others confirmed Axelrod himself had "an even more significant role – that he leaked the initial story."

Like the Ryans, Hull and his ex-wife both objected to releasing their sealed divorce records, but no matter. Less than three weeks before the primary, in a candidates debate,

Hull was forced to defend himself against charges he was a domestic abuser – his ex-wife had "kicked me in the leg," he explained, "and I hit her shin to try to get her to not continue to kick me" – and he went on to receive a mere ten percent of the vote as Obama surged to the nomination.

This was politics the Obama way, the rule-twisting contempt for the electoral process that is by now second nature in his party.

It goes all the way back to his first political race. Even then, the filthiest of dirty tricks was his stock in trade.

In 1996, having just directed a successful voter registration drive, Obama was ready to move up. At the time, he was heavily dependent on his wife's salary. His own source of income came from a business he had created initiating civil rights lawsuits and from his position as a lecturer at the University of Chicago. Through his years as an activist working in the projects, he'd gotten his feet wet in the forest of Chicago politics, and he'd nailed down a few key alliances. Obama planned to use these connections as a state senate seat in Obama's part of town was coming open. The incumbent was a woman named Alice Palmer. A pedigreed socialist with many of the same connections he had, Palmer was giving up her seat in the Illinois legislature to run for Congress since the incumbent in *that* race, Mel Reynolds, had been forced to resign after a conviction for scx crimes.

This was the Obama campaign that was infamously launched in Bill Ayers and Bernadine Dohrn's living room.

But it wouldn't actually be much of a campaign because Obama systematically knocked out every single one of his opponents by seeing to it their ballot petitions were invalidated. That included those of Alice Palmer, the incumbent, who after losing to Jesse Jackson, Jr. in the primary to succeed Reynolds, had decided to run for re-election.

Since Obama was allegedly a Palmer ally, with nearly identical politics, Palmer asked him to step aside. His campaign's response was to pore over her hastily-gathered ballot petitions, successfully challenging enough signatures to keep her off the ballot.

"I liked Alice Palmer a lot. I thought she was a good public servant," Obama said later. "It was very awkward. That part of it I wish had played out entirely differently."

Obama proceeded to challenge the signatures of his three remaining opponents one by one until all of *them* were also forced from the ballot. If a name had been printed rather than signed in cursive, it was thrown out; and, so too, if a signature was valid but the person who'd gathered it wasn't properly registered; and the search for technical irregularities went on. In the case of one rival, Gha-is Askia, more than 1,800 signatures had been turned in, for a requirement of 757. By the time Obama's team was through with him he was 69 signatures short.

"Why say you're for a new tomorrow, then do old-style Chicago politics to remove legitimate candidates?" demanded Askia, to a *Tribune* reporter. "He talks about honor and democracy, but what honor is there in getting rid of every other candidate so you can run scot-free? Why not let the people decide?"

Obama's response? "To my mind, we were just abiding by the rules that had been set up. I gave some thought to ... should people be on the ballot even if they didn't meet the requirements. My conclusion was that if you couldn't run a successful petition drive, then that raised questions in terms of how effective a representative you were going to be."

In the overwhelmingly Democrat 13th legislative District, Obama faced only a weak Republican candidate in the general, and he received 82 percent of the vote.

Asked whether the methods he used hadn't denied voters a real choice, his answer was: "I think they ended up with a very good state senator."

"We actually ran a terrific campaign up until the point we knew that we weren't going to have to appear on the ballot with anybody," Obama later said, without evident irony. "I mean, we had prepared for it. We had raised money. We had tons of volunteers. There was enormous enthusiasm."

But the fact is, Obama would have been beaten badly if he'd had to run against Palmer.

In fairness, this *was* Chicago, which is to say, it's not like Obama pioneered such tactics. Nonetheless, there is obvious irony in that Obama presented himself as a pro-democracy reformer. And though he "may have gotten his start registering thousands of voters," as observes the veteran observer of Windy City politics John Kass, "in that first race, he made sure voters had just one choice."

When the seat came up again in 1998, thanks to the strange rules providing for irregular terms surrounding census years, Obama got 89 percent of the vote. In 2000 and 2002 he ran unopposed.

But, of course, Obama's ambitions went far beyond Springfield, and even as he held fast to his state senate seat, in 2000 he'd sensed opportunity, and challenged incumbent Congressman Bobby Rush in the Democratic primary.

Rush had been the founder of the Illinois chapter of the Black Panther Party, making him a longtime prominent figure in black Chicago politics, but he'd run against Richard Daley for mayor in 1999 and gotten just 28 percent of the vote, signaling he might be vulnerable.

But Bobby Rush's ballot petitions couldn't be invalidated. Obama would have to win a fair fight, under circumstances that didn't favor him, and his odds grew even longer in October 1999, when Rush's son Huey was shot and killed, engendering a wave of popular sympathy. In response to Huey Rush's murder, the Illinois legislature took up a raft of gun control bills that had previously been invalidated by the state Supreme Court. Though Obama supported the bills, he missed a crucial vote, and a key measure failed by five votes. Valid as his explanation was – he was in Hawaii visiting his mother, expecting the legislature to suspend business for the holiday season – Obama came under fire for his absence.

At the same time, Rush, long practiced in the politics of racial grievance, was blasting the smooth-talking Obama as inauthentic. "Barack Obama went to Harvard and became an educated fool," he declared. "We're not impressed with these folks with these Eastern elite degrees. Barack is a person who read about the civil-rights protests and thinks he knows all about it."

Obama was cooked. On primary day, Rush spanked him by a 61-30 margin.

It was in the aftermath of this unaccustomed humiliation that Obama turbocharged his association with Jeremiah Wright, ingratiating himself with the South Chicago black community to ensure that he would never again be called, as third-place contender in the race Donne Trotter termed him, a "white man in blackface."

Indeed, that pledge was the flip side of another vow made by a different kind of racist in the wake of his losing a primary race in 1950's Alabama. "I will never," declared George Wallace, "be out-niggered again."

In practical terms, Obama now found himself obliged to undertake a far-from-simple political balancing act. On the one hand, in order to maintain his viability as a potential national candidate, he had to take care in his role as a state legislator to avoid casting votes that might later mark him as too far out of the mainstream – and, indeed, he was a very ordinary left-centrist Democrat in the Illinois Senate, often voting "present" and known, to the degree he was at all, for long-winded speechifying on the floor.

Likewise, as a lecturer at the University of Chicago during these years, he did the absolute minimum to hold onto his job. He wrote nothing and participated little in the intellectual life of the university. His colleague, the conservative-libertarian Richard Epstein, a close observer of Obama, later suggested this was likely a reaction to the ill fortune suffered by leftist law professor Lani Guinier who, after her 1993 nomination by Bill Clinton as assistant attorney general for civil rights, got dumped after opponents discovered she'd left a paper trail of writings on ways to reconfigure the electoral system to increase the number of minority officeholders. Epstein saw Guinier's experience as a pointed example to Obama "not to put his name to anything that could haunt him politically."

Yet at the same time, such a strategy not only ran counter to his need to please his overwhelmingly black constituency, it was a betrayal of his own deeply felt leftist beliefs. For as he sat in the pews of Trinity United Church all those years, listening to Reverend Wright's sermons, he likely agreed with most every word.

Still, only occasionally would he publicly betray that side of himself. One notable instance involved his collaboration with Bill Ayers on juvenile justice. "Knowing that Illinois was headed for a major reform of its juvenile crime laws," notes Stanley Kurtz, Ayers wrote "a blistering critique of the Illinois juvenile justice system. Ayers was following the lead of his wife and former Weatherman leader, Bernardine Dohrn, who had founded and directed the Children and Family Justice Center at Northwestern University...."

How unhinged was – and is – the former Weatherman terrorist on crime? According to Kurtz, "Ayers opposes trying even the most vicious juvenile murderers as adults," arguing "prisons impose conformity and obedience on society, falsely causing us to distinguish between 'normal' and 'deviant' behavior... He also pointedly compares America's juvenile justice system to the mass detention of a generation of young blacks under South African apartheid."

He adds that "Ayers, Dohrn, and Obama were very arguably the three most powerful voices in Illinois opposed to the modest strengthening of the state's juvenile justice laws debated and finally passed in 1997–98," though "Obama understood perfectly well that the views of this famously radical couple on both crime and American society were virtually unchanged from their Weatherman days."

Obama fought a bill that would introduce "blended" sentencing for the worst juvenile offenders. But, when it was apparent it would pass overwhelmingly, he strategically dropped his opposition. He was also one of only three Illinois state senators to vote against a proposal making it a criminal offense for convicts on probation or bail to have contact with a street gang. And he annually brought bills aimed at stopping police from "racially profiling" black people.

In this regard, an article Obama wrote for his neighborhood weekly, the *Hyde Park Herald,* is of note. "Racial profiling may explain why incarceration rates are so high among young African-Americans — law enforcement officials may be targeting blacks and other minorities as potential criminals and are using the Vehicle Code as a tool to stop and search them."

There was likely an element of truth to this then, as there might be even today. But to assert that the alarmingly high rates of predatory black criminality are primarily due to systemic racism is to willfully ignore the key matters of behavior and personal responsibility, and to peddle the false and condescending notion that blacks are less capable than other Americans of adhering to high standards. It is also to ignore the most likely victims of predator black criminals: other black people. But these beliefs are ones that Obama would carry into the Oval Office, and to his control over the Justice Department, repeatedly expounding them from the bully pulpit. Among its other horrific consequences, it would engender the so-called "Soros DA's" – among many others, New York's Alvin Bragg, Philadelphia's Larry Krasner, and Kim Foxx in Obama's adopted hometown of Chicago—who would refuse to enforce the laws on the books as a matter of high principle.

Too, as an up-and-coming Democratic pol, Obama joined the board of the left-wing Woods Fund, which dispensed money to a variety of supposedly noble leftist causes, even as he simultaneously got plugged into the network of profitable "friendships" known euphemistically as the Chicago Way. Among these was his association with the land baron and restaurant franchisee Tony Rezko, who would contribute more than a quarter-million dollars to his campaigns before being indicted on wire fraud, bribery, money laundering, and attempted extortion charges in a scheme to extort millions from businesses seeking contracts with the Illinois Teachers System Board and the Illinois Health Facilities Planning Board. By amazing coincidence, at one point Rezko's wife purchased a lot in the Kenwood district of Chicago on the very day the Obamas bought the house next door for some $300,000 below market. All involved earnestly swore this was no back-room bribe, and Obama, by this time a U.S. Senator, averred "it was a mistake to have been engaged with him at all in this or any other personal business dealing that would allow him, or anyone else, to believe he had done me a favor."

Another Chicago friend of Obama (and Rezko) was Dr. Eric Whitaker, whom Obama originally met when both were at Harvard, and to whom as State Senator Obama he gave what he himself termed a "glowing" reference, helping Whitaker secure the position of state health commissioner. In that role, Whitaker sent millions to black churches on programs to educate minorities about AIDS, breast cancer and potential public health emergencies. The agency then got caught up in scandal when the Illinois Health Facilities Planning Board was used by Rezko and his associates to solicit kickbacks and payoffs on medical construction projects.

Whitaker subsequently moved on to run the University of Chicago's Urban Health Initiative. This was a program started by Michelle Obama, who made $317,000 per year as the hospital's vice president. Its main function was to engage in patient-dumping – shooing poor patients without private health insurance to other hospitals so they could save on expenses. Michelle also hired Axelrod's PR firm to sell that plan to the people of the South Side.

All in all, by Chicago Way standards, it was typical enough. But it anticipated how Obama as president would encourage the moral corruption of his minions in the IRS and Justice Department; and, too, the ways the Obamas, like the Clintons before them, would shamelessly monetize their post-presidency.

Equally ominous in its implications for the nation's future was the cynical contempt for democratic processes evident in Obama's savaging of his early political opponents.

During the 1980s, Ronald Reagan and Democratic House Speaker Tip O'Neill could be bitter ideological foes, yet at the end of the business day get together for a beer. No more. Now political opponents were to be cast as morally reprehensible. And their defeat was to be accomplished by any means necessary.

Thus it was that Obama brought to national politics a new rapacity to win any cost: to lie, and cheat, and savage political foes, no matter the lasting damage.

Yet even as he took care to protect his political viability in his public positioning on the issues, the rising pol faced another, and more sinister, challenge: speculation – not all of it generated by political opponents – involving his sexuality.

At a time when polls showed that even most Democratic voters regarded homosexuality as aberrant, and gay marriage was not yet even a blip on the radar, such allegations would likely have been fatal to Obama's nascent political career.

Yet, both because the rumors seemed so implausible – and because his opponents lacked Obama's well-honed killer instinct – they received no public notice.

That remained the case over the next twenty years, through Obama's service in the Illinois State Senate and his term in the U.S. Senate and, indeed, into his run for the presidency.

This might have changed on December 24, 2007, when Donald Young, Trinity Church's gay choir director and the subject of some of the most graphic rumors, was found dead in his hotel room of multiple gunshot wounds. But by then his media Praetorian Guard was already in place, poised to run interference on Reverend Wright; and even had they not been, the story and its potential implications would have been too hot to touch. it remained almost entirely confined to the backwaters of the internet.

Sixteen years later, Donald Young's murder remains unsolved.

On July 17, 2010, the supermarket tabloid *The Globe* published an interview with Young's mother. "What was the cause of my son's death?" Norma Jean Young asked in *the* interview. "I'm very suspicious that it may have been related to Obama. Donald and Obama were very close friends. Whatever went on with this is very private. I am suspicious of a cover-up!"

That, too, was almost universally ignored.

It was not until the 2017, and the revelation by historian David Garrow in his book *Rising Star* of a November of a

1982 letter from the future president to his Occidental College girlfriend, that the subject of Obama's sexuality received some limited currency. "You see, " Obama wrote the girlfriend, Alex McNear, "I make love to men, but in the imagination…My mind is androgynous to a great extent and I hope to make it more so until I can think in terms of people, not women as opposed to men."

All that aside, what is beyond question is that the vitriol, ruthlessness and to-the-death ideological warfare Obama deployed from the earliest days of his political career is now embedded in almost every sphere of American life, with the nation mired in a spiritual ugliness unsurpassed since the run up to the Civil War.

The left has long been well-versed in slander. Like Muslim zealots dealing with infidels, committed radicals like Obama believe that any act, and certainly any untruth, is justified in defense of the faith. And Obama would usher in an era where his friends and supporters would come to define their opponents in the very terms favored by Frank Marshall Davis and others of the Old Left: as "bigots" or "fascists."

Obama's capacity for bare-knuckled indecency was already apparent in the 2008 election campaign, when his team busily spread dirt on Sarah Palin's marriage and dished rumors of John McCain's alleged affair; and, if not then, when he knee-capped the Tea Party movement by siccing the IRS on its leaders.

But surely its most perfect distillation was what Obama's attack dog Harry Reid did to Mitt Romney in 2012, taking to the Senate floor to accuse the hapless GOP nominee of not having paid taxes for ten years. "Let him prove that he has paid taxes," he bellowed, "because he hasn't."

It was a shameless lie, and a provable one, as Romney's tax returns soon showed. But no matter. Reid doubled down, asserting, "People who make as much money as Mitt Romney have many tricks at their disposal to avoid paying taxes…When it comes to answering the legitimate questions the American people have about whether he avoided paying his fair share in taxes or why he opened a Swiss bank account, Romney has shut up…"

It was appalling at the time, and it is even more so today, watching the likes of Adam Schiff and Joe Biden issue forth false claims which are even more brazen and inflammatory as Chicago-style Democrat politics metastasizes into the American status quo.

Yet later, when Reid was called on it, his breezy response might as well have come from his sponsor's own lips.

"Romney didn't win, did he?"

CHAPTER 7

THE MAGIC NEGRO

"I am absolutely certain that generations from now," Obama declared in his acceptance speech at the 2008 Democratic National Convention in Denver, in that easy, grandiose cadence of his, "we will be able to look back and tell our children that this was the moment when we began to provide care for the sick and good jobs to the jobless; this was the moment when the rise of the oceans began to slow and our planet began to heal; this was the moment when we ended a war and secured our nation and restored our image as the last, best hope on earth."

This was the Obama who seemed destined to cast away all the old rules and assumptions about American politics. This was Obama transcendent, about to emerge as a deeply transformational president. This was, above all, the Obama who would smash all racial barriers.

That's what tens of millions voters chose to believe, anyway, across the political spectrum.

His political guru David Axelrod called Obama "Black Jesus" and said, "he is the living, breathing apotheosis of the American melting pot."

How could such a sleazy Chicago pol emerge from the ooze of his Alinskyite South Side agitation and bad-faith political campaigns, as this supposedly soaring, untouchable figure?

Because Obama was presented as something new and remarkable, and the deliverer of America from its shameful past. Such a figure could not be disparaged, or be subject to the sort of media scrutiny that had only lately torched more conventional Democrat presidential hopefuls like Gary Hart and John Edwards.

Because Obama was the "Magic Negro."

Los Angeles Times film critic David Ehrenstein, who is himself of mixed racial background, says that the Magic Negro "is a figure of postmodern folk culture, coined by snarky 20th century sociologists, to explain a cultural figure who emerged in the wake of *Brown vs. Board of Education*... He's there to assuage white 'guilt' (i.e., the minimal discomfort they feel) over the role of slavery and racial segregation in American history, while replacing stereotypes of a dangerous, highly sexualized black man with a benign figure for whom interracial sexual congress holds no interest."

Ehrenstein noted that the Magic Negro is known mostly as a cinematic trope – naming such illustrious black actors as Sidney Poitier, Morgan Freeman and Will Smith, in films like *Lilies of the Field*, *To Sir, With Love*, *Guess Who's Coming to Dinner*, *Driving Miss Daisy*, and *The Legend of Bagger Vance*. In every case, the characters they play exude wisdom and quiet nobility.

Obama, said Ehrenstein, was a sensation precisely because he was the political incarnation of the movie device – a Magic Negro to heal America as Bagger Vance would heal Runnulph Junuh's golf game.

He continued…

"The only mud that momentarily stuck was criticism (white and black alike) concerning Obama's alleged 'inauthenticity,' as compared to such sterling examples of 'genuine' blackness as Al Sharpton and Snoop Dogg."

Yet Ehrenstein said that ultimately that very "inauthenticity" worked for Obama. Because he wasn't seen as fully black, because he could point (whether truthfully or not) to a Kenyan lineage rather than one derived from black slaves, because he'd been raised at least partially in another country, Barack Obama was the sort of world citizen white liberals aspire to be. "Like a comic-book superhero, Obama is there to help, out of the sheer goodness of a heart we need not know or understand."

Indeed, from the start it was white liberals who embraced Obama with special fervor, even if in 2008 that meant deserting their longtime favorite, Hillary Clinton.

And over the years to come, that devotion to Obama and his policies would never flag, even when it meant suspending the very beliefs and standards that had long defined liberalism itself, from the commitment to a colorblind society to respect for the views of those with whom one disagreed. So bound would bedazzled liberals be to Obama and Obamaism – so essential would their devotion be to their self-image as good and caring people – that any criticism of the man or his policies *had* to be racist. And as the policies floundered and failed, and for millions of others the disillusion with Obama grew, so did their sense of outrage and moral certainty; so much so that they too would likewise soon wholeheartedly embrace the propositions that young Barack had imbibed from his mentors: that America is fundamentally and intractably racist, its history of white supremacy ongoing into the present, and that those who believed otherwise had been fraudulently educated. To excuse Obama's manifest failures and ideological deceptions, they had to turn not against their hero, but against America itself.

But all that was yet to come. In the midst of the 2008 campaign the ex-community organizer was only on step one of pulling off the con job of the century, selling himself as a healer.

And when there arose the great challenge to that narrative in the person of Reverend Jeremiah Wright, Obama used his "More Perfect Union" speech into an act of astonishing political jujitsu.

To this day, the speech is lauded by the Obama claque in the media as akin to Lincoln's "House Divided" address; clearer-eyed observers even then recognized what it showed above all was Obama's faith in the credulity of the American electorate.

Nonetheless, so vital was it in the making of Obama's legend, so elaborate was it in the quality of its manipulation and sheer two-facedness, so ultimately representative of the man and his character, that it merits further parsing.

Obama began with a paean to the American founding.

"Two hundred and twenty-one years ago, in a hall that still stands across the street, a group of men gathered and, with these simple words, launched America's improbable experiment in democracy. Farmers and scholars; statesmen and patriots who had traveled across an ocean to escape tyranny and persecution finally made real their declaration of independence at a Philadelphia convention that lasted through the spring of 1787.

"The document they produced was eventually signed but ultimately unfinished. It was stained by this nation's original sin of slavery, a question that divided the colonies and brought the convention to a stalemate until the founders chose to allow the slave trade to continue for at least 20 more years, and to leave any final resolution to future generations."

This was something Frank Marshall Davis did often in his columns, bathing himself in the afterglow of the Founding Fathers: an especially smart move in a speech aimed at putting the Jeremiah Wright issue to bed. It is the ultimate irony that a dozen years hence, as a result of his tenure at the country's helm, and the *New York Times' 1619 Project* it spawned, no Democrat (and too few Republicans) would dare begin with so unqualified a celebration of the Founders.

The speech moves on to the unfulfilled promises of the Constitution, through the Civil War and the ongoing battle for civil rights, Obama now putting himself in the tradition of the great civil rights leaders of the past.

"This was one of the tasks we set forth at the beginning of this campaign - to continue the long march of those who came before us, a march for a more just, more equal, more free, more caring and more prosperous America.

"I chose to run for the presidency at this moment in history because I believe deeply that we cannot solve the challenges of our time unless we solve them together - unless we perfect our union by understanding that we may have different stories, but we hold common hopes; that we may not look the same and we may not have come from the same place, but we all want to move in the same direction - towards a better future for our children and our grandchildren."

Of course, the communist Old Left likewise did everything it could to define itself as the defender of civil liberties and the oppressed minorities. Indeed, knowing what was to come – the man's reflexively divisive rhetoric on race; his endless casting of group against group; his administration's promotion of indoctrination over history in the nation's schools – the impulse to gag here may be forgiven.

He next moved on to his own story – the version presented in *Dreams From My Father*.

"I am the son of a black man from Kenya and a white woman from Kansas. I was raised with the help of a white grandfather who survived a Depression to serve in Patton's Army during World War II and a white grandmother who worked on a bomber assembly line at Fort Leavenworth while he was overseas. I've gone to some of the best schools in America and lived in one of the world's poorest nations. I am married to a black American who carries within her the blood of slaves and slaveowners - an inheritance we pass on to our two precious daughters. I have brothers, sisters, nieces, nephews, uncles and cousins, of every race and every hue, scattered across three continents, and for as long as I live, I will never forget that in no other country on Earth is my story even possible.

"It's a story that hasn't made me the most conventional candidate. But it is a story that has seared into my genetic makeup the idea that this nation is more than the sum of its parts - that out of many, we are truly one…And yet, it has only been in the last couple of weeks that the discussion of race in this campaign has taken a particularly divisive turn."

And it was on to…

"…my former pastor, Reverend Jeremiah Wright, use incendiary language to express views that have the potential not only to widen the racial divide, but views that denigrate both the greatness and the goodness of our nation; that rightly offend white and black alike.

"I have already condemned, in unequivocal terms, the statements of Reverend Wright that have caused such controversy. For some, nagging questions remain. Did I know him to be an occasionally fierce critic of American domestic and foreign policy? Of course. Did I ever hear him make remarks that could be considered controversial while I sat in church? Yes. Did I strongly disagree with many of his political views? Absolutely - just as I'm sure many of you have heard remarks from your pastors, priests, or rabbis with which you strongly disagreed.

"But the remarks that have caused this recent firestorm weren't simply controversial. They weren't simply a religious leader's effort to speak out against perceived injustice. Instead, they expressed a profoundly distorted view of this country - a view that sees white racism as endemic, and that elevates what is wrong with America above all that we know is right with America; a view that sees the conflicts in the Middle East as rooted primarily in the actions of stalwart allies like Israel, instead of emanating from the perverse and hateful ideologies of radical Islam."

Where to start? EVERYTHING about this is a lie. While Obama had condemned a couple of Wright's remarks appearing in *Rolling Stone*, he had *never* before repudiated Wright's overall worldview – something that earlier in the campaign might have risked alienating significant portions of the black electorate.

White racism as *not* endemic, in Obama's view? "Stalwart allies" like Israel? Not merely lies, but what would soon register as such laughably contemptible ones.

A bit further along, even as he justifies his own many years listening to Reverend Wright's viciously anti-white sermons, he offers white liberals the *frisson* of an insider take on the inner city black experience.

"Like other predominantly black churches across the country, Trinity embodies the black community in its entirety - the doctor and the welfare mom, the model student and the former gang-banger. Like other black churches, Trinity's services are full of raucous laughter and sometimes bawdy humor. They are full of dancing, clapping, screaming and shouting that may seem jarring to the untrained ear. The church contains in full the kindness and cruelty, the fierce intelligence and the shocking ignorance, the struggles and successes, the love and yes, the bitterness and bias that make up the black experience in America.

"And this helps explain, perhaps, my relationship with Reverend Wright. As imperfect as he may be, he has been like family to me. He strengthened my faith, officiated my wedding and baptized my children. Not once in my conversations with him have I heard him talk about any ethnic group in derogatory terms, or treat whites with whom he interacted with anything but courtesy and respect. He contains within him the contradictions - the good and the bad - of the community that he has served diligently for so many years."

On and on it goes. After Wright goes under the bus, so, famously, does "my white grandmother - a woman who helped raise me, a woman who sacrificed again and again for me, a woman who loves me as much as she loves anything in this world, but a woman who once confessed her fear of black men who passed by her on the street, and who on more than one occasion has uttered racial or ethnic stereotypes that made me cringe."

So, no, he allows, he's not *really* disavowing anyone, just reminding us that the history of race in America is as deeply complicated as it is heartbreakingly painful. But – the central point, hammered away at in a dozen ways – we must talk about all this openly, without fear of censure. And – unspoken, but obvious – he is the man to make that discussion happen, and bring us to the future of genuine equality pre-ordained by the founders.

It was, from a man who would go on to shut down all honest conversation about race in America, and cast those who took positions contrary to the left's as racists, a bravura performance, jaw-dropping in its (that favorite Obama word) audacity.

"Other blacks may hate you," was his reassuring message to white people. "And they have good reason. But while I understand why they do, that isn't me."

The speech continues…

"…But I have asserted a firm conviction - a conviction rooted in my faith in God and my faith in the American people - that working together we can move beyond some of our old racial wounds," he proclaimed, heading for the home stretch, " and that in fact we have no choice if we are to continue on the path of a more perfect union.

"For the African-American community, that path means embracing the burdens of our past without becoming victims of our past. It means continuing to insist on a full measure of justice in every aspect of American life. But it also means binding our particular grievances - for better health care, and better schools, and better jobs - to the larger aspirations of all Americans - the white woman struggling to break the glass ceiling, the white man who's been laid off, the immigrant trying to feed his family. And it means taking full responsibility for our own lives - by demanding more from our fathers, and spending more time with our children, and reading to them, and teaching them that while they may face challenges and discrimination in their own lives, they must never succumb to despair or cynicism; they must always believe that they can write their own destiny...The profound mistake of Reverend Wright's sermons is not that he spoke about racism in our society. It's that he spoke as if our society was static; as if no progress has been made; as if this country - a country that has made it possible for one of his own members to run for the highest office in the land and build a coalition of white and black; Latino and Asian, rich and poor, young and old - is still irrevocably bound to a tragic past. But what we know - what we have seen - is that America can change. That is true genius of this nation. What we have already achieved gives us hope - the audacity to hope - for what we can and must achieve tomorrow…For we have a choice in this country. We can accept a politics that breeds division, and conflict, and cynicism. We can tackle race only as spectacle - as we did in the OJ trial - or in the wake of tragedy, as we did in the aftermath of Katrina - or as fodder for the nightly news. We can play Reverend Wright's sermons on every channel, every day and talk about them from now until the election, and make the only question in this campaign whether or not the American people think that I somehow believe or sympathize with his most offensive words. We can pounce on some gaffe by a Hillary supporter as evidence that she's playing the race card, or we can speculate on whether white men will all flock to John McCain in the general election regardless of his policies.

"We can do that.

"But if we do, I can tell you that in the next election, we'll be talking about some other distraction. And then another one. And then another one. And nothing will change."

In fact, in the next election Barack Obama's campaign talked about Mitt Romney as a sexist and misogynist over his awkward "binders full of women" statement in a debate, or dining out on Romney's hidden-video statement about the 47 percent of Americans who don't pay income tax.

But for political distractions, he would have been a one-term president.

"That is one option. Or, at this moment, in this election, we can come together and say: 'Not this time.' This time we want to talk about the crumbling schools that are stealing the future of black children and white children and Asian children and Hispanic children and Native American children. This time we want to reject the cynicism that tells us that these kids can't learn; that those kids who don't look like us are somebody else's problem. The children of America are not those kids, they are our kids, and we will not let them fall behind in a 21st-century economy. Not this time.

"…This time we want to talk about the men and women of every color and creed who serve together, and fight together and bleed together under the same proud flag… And as so many generations have come to realize over the course of the 221 years since a band of patriots signed that document in Philadelphia, that is where the perfection begins."

The irony in this strikes with particular force. In the America he'd go on to remake, those patriots, almost to a man, would be canceled.

It's not that Obama fooled everyone, not even on the left.

The black writer Ta-Nehisi Coates, for one, had little use for Obama's take on race relations. "It rests on the notion that the black community, more than other communities, is characterized by a bunch of hapless layabouts who spend their days ticking off reparations demands and shaking their fist at the white man," he wrote presciently. "The truth is that the dominant conversation in the black community today is not about racism or victimization but about self-improvement. . . . in terms of their outlook, their belief in hard work and family, African Americans aren't any different from white Americans."

Nonetheless, the speech put a dent in the Jeremiah Wright problem, and little more than a month later after he disavowed Wright in a way he said in Philadelphia he couldn't do, Obama would finish off a Hillary Clinton who'd seemingly lacked the guts to go after him for his longtime racist and radical connections.

Then, again, Hillary – who in any case, believed many of the same things – might not have been wrong in supposing doing so wouldn't have mattered. For already Obama was changing the mindset of traditional liberals, turning associations that in the past had been politically poisonous to mere afterthoughts; liberals, that is, who were already unknowingly *en route* to embracing much of the old Communist Party USA narrative about America.

These were the people who wielded the greatest sway in both the party and the country, and they had no problem with any of it.

In fact, it would be less than a month after the "More Perfect Union" speech, on April 12, that Obama would tell a group of well-heeled progressives in what he thought was a private setting what he really thought of the white working class voters that traditionally constituted the Democrats' base: that they "get bitter, they cling to guns or religion or antipathy to people who aren't like them or anti-immigrant sentiment or anti-trade sentiment as a way to explain their frustrations."

John McCain's campaign against Obama in the general election went on to be one of the most gutless, incompetent and lifeless efforts in American history. Not only did McCain fail to go after Obama on the Wright issue – again, for fear of being falsely labeled a bigot – but he failed to capitalize on his own history of five years' residence at the Hanoi Hilton, tortured by men who believed many of the same things his opponent did.

It was obvious, McCain was the fall guy for the anointed one, Barack Hussein Obama.

CHAPTER 8

CRITICAL RACE THEORY AND THE WOKE MIND VIRUS

I n researching his book *The Communist*, Paul Kengor contacted John Drew, the fellow-traveling leftist and now-conservative (owing to the triumph of experience over youthful passion) who, as a student at Occidental College, was briefly in Barack Obama's social circle, and in October 2010 Kengor interviewed Drew for a podcast on the subject of his relationship with the then-college sophomore Obama.

"I can definitely kick down some doors here intellectually by nailing down that he [Obama] had a very consistent ideology," said Drew, "probably from the time that he was [in Hawaii] until he was there with Alice Palmer and Bill Ayers in Chicago. I think his current behavior demonstrates that he does still have these ideological convictions. Whenever he talks about taxing the richest two percent, I think even though he knows that will harm the economy—to him, that redistribution of wealth is still extremely important. And I think the problem here is that he never studied political science or economics the way I did. He just went straight to law school. … He never had any real business experience, never had a payroll to meet, and I think he still is locked in a very dangerous mindset where I think if he didn't fight to redistribute the wealth, he would feel guilty—as if he were violating a John Rawls *Theory of Justice* ideology…

"I think whenever he talks about people clinging to their guns and their religion due to economic stress, that's just the standard Marxist argument. In fact, that's the argument of alienation and class-consciousness that [Marxists believe that people] hold to, the superficial religious and cultural ideals of the capitalist culture. [Marxists believe that people hold to that] instead of paying attention to the root economic changes, which are supposedly controlling their thoughts and their behavior. So, he's still using the Marxist mental architecture in the way he talks about things, and I really think he's surrounded by people that share that mental architecture."

In college, Drew himself was a Marxist, but what he learned and saw studying abroad, at the University of Sussex, and then at graduate school at Cornell, convinced him that Marx's predicted proletarian revolution would never come, and he graduated to a more subtle form of Marxism – the cultural Marxism preached by the academics of the Frankfurt School like Herbert Marcuse, Theodor Adorno, Max Hork-heimer and Erich Fromm. They believed that the fundamental changes in society sought by the left would ultimately be achieved through changes in the institutions governing society, starting with the schools and moving into every other meaningful sphere of daily life.

At the time, recalled Drew, young Barack Obama was having none of that talk. He said Drew's prognostication that the revolution of the proletariat was not on the horizon was "crazy."

"Since I was a Marxist myself at the time, and had studied variations in Marxist theory," Drew noted, "I can state that everything I heard Obama argue that evening was consistent with Marxist philosophy, including the ideas that class struggle was leading to an inevitable revolution, and that an elite group of revolutionaries was needed to lead the effort. If he had not been a true Marxist-Leninist, I would have noticed and remembered. I can still, with some degree of ideological precision, identify which students at Occidental College were radicals and which ones were not."

Drew believes he ultimately won the argument, and that he might actually have helped pull Obama off the path of violent revolution and toward electoral politics the night of their memorable back and forth.

Because, of course, Drew was right. The history of communist revolutions is they never happen the way that Karl Marx predicted, with an uprising of the proletariat fueled by economic dissatisfaction. To the contrary, experience teaches that for a revolution to succeed, two elements are essential: that a nation's underpinnings have already been seriously weakened, perhaps by external forces; and that the revolutionaries have come to dominate its sustaining cultural institutions.

This, in essence, is the story of why, for all the fervor of the Frank Marshall Davises and Paul Robesons, they and theirs could never succeed in stoking Soviet-style revolution in America or any other of the more prosperous nations of the Western world. And how, rather than taking the failure of the Marxist movement as a repudiation of their beliefs, the West's intellectual left returned to the drawing board. The result was what would evolve into the woke tyranny of the current age.

In a more personal sense, it is also the story of Barack Obama's radical journey from the wild-eyed revolutionary John Drew encountered in California to the corporatist citizen of the world whose deep-seated leftism was sufficiently hidden that even as he set America aflame on front after front, he was widely portrayed as a "centrist."

The most influential of the early cultural Marxists was an Italian communist named Antonio Gramsci, whose famous formulation of the "march through the institutions" describes the international left in the West today. Gramsci's insight was that three elements underpinned the success of Western democracy: Christianity, nationalism, and charity.

For the dreamed-of revolution to succeed, all three had to be destroyed.

"Socialism is precisely the religion that must overwhelm Christianity," he wrote. "In the new order, Socialism will triumph by first capturing the culture via infiltration of schools, universities, churches and the media by transforming the consciousness of society."

It hardly need be said that this pretty much encapsulates the social collapse afoot in contemporary America.

Gramsci fell afoul of Benito Mussolini, the fascist Italian dictator who appreciated only some of the construct he'd presented. Mussolini wasn't much for trashing nationalism, as nationalism was the source of his political power, and he had Gramsci sent to prison, where he died in 1937. But his ideas outlived him, having taken particular root in the early 1920's at Germany's Institute of Social Research at the University of Frankfurt, in what came to be known as the Frankfurt School.

Once Adolf Hitler and the Nazis came to power in Germany in the early 1930's – infused with the same militant nationalist ideal as Mussolini but also consumed by psychopathic hatred of the Other – the overwhelmingly Jewish intellectuals of the Frankfurt School fled their homeland, lest they suffer the same fate as Gramsci. Many made their way to America, especially to New York, where more than a few found teaching positions at the New School for Social Research and Columbia University.

As Stanley Kurtz noted in his book *Radical-In-Chief*, very little information is known about Obama's time at Columbia, where he transferred after two years at Occidental. This is surely not an accident. While he's never released transcripts from any of his college or post-graduate institutions, at Columbia almost nobody even seems to remember him. Obama's own less-than-convincing explanation is that he spent his hours reading books rather than socializing.

The Las Vegas oddsmaker and conservative columnist Wayne Allyn Root was a contemporary of Obama's at Columbia, and Root says he would have taken many of the same classes Obama needed in order to earn his political science degree. Yet Root has no memory of Obama.

"If anyone should have questions about Obama's record at Columbia University, it's me," Root wrote in a column which originally appeared in *The Blaze*. "We both graduated (according to Obama) Columbia University, Class of '83. We were both (according to Obama) Pre-Law and Political Science majors. And I thought I knew most everyone at Columbia. I certainly thought I'd heard of all of my fellow Political Science majors. But not Obama (or as he was known then- Barry Soetoro). I never met him. Never saw him. Never even heard of him. And none of the classmates that I knew at Columbia has ever met him, saw him, or heard of him.

"But don't take my word for it. The *Wall Street Journal* reported in 2008 that Fox News randomly called 400 of our Columbia classmates and never found one who had ever met Obama."

Root's theory was that Obama gamed the system at both Occidental and Columbia, and then at Harvard Law School, by identifying himself as a foreign student from Indonesia, and barely went to class and barely graduated. That's why he would never release his transcripts.

Kurtz believes Obama found his way as a Marxist with a future after attending a conference put on in April of 1983 by the Democratic Socialists of America at New York's Cooper Union in New York. Per Kurtz, community organizing, particularly in the black community, was the central focus of that Socialist Scholars Conference, with multiple panel discussions covering best practices of organizing minority and disadvantaged groups along socialist lines.

Following an opening address by Professor Frances Fox Piven, the keynote speaker was Michael Harrington, America's leading socialist of the time, whose works had inspired LBJ's War On Poverty, which sent trillions of dollars down the drain on a raft of government programs. Harrington ultimately soured on the War On Poverty as a half-measure, and by the time of his 1983 address to the Socialist Scholars Conference, he was touting a new brand of socialism – one built on community organizing among the "black and brown" people.

Kurtz sums up Harrington's evolving doctrine this way:

"As his thought developed from the sixties through the eighties, Harrington increasingly turned away from classic socialist plans for nationalization of the economy. Instead, he embraced a gradualist program in which workers and community groups would gain control of industries from within, redistributing wealth along the way. For Harrington, union ownership of a company, or reserved seats for community organizations on boards of directors or public utility commissions, was democracy and was socialism. So even in the event of a violent revolution (which with luck would never be necessary), Harrington believed that community-controlled wealth redistribution would effectively guarantee democracy in a post-revolutionary world. By the eighties, then, Harrington looked less to a socialist central government than to a consortium of unions and community organizations (for example, ACORN in its dealings with banks) to act as guardians of a genuine people's democracy. Of course, treating community groups like ACORN or its affiliated SEIU union locals as guardians of decentralized 'democracy' in a socialized state will strike many as the very opposite of democracy as Americans understand that term. Yet by 1983, Harrington's [Democratic Socialists of America] DSA was embracing this vision of a grassroots-based socialism."

Here's a direct quote from Harrington's speech: "We must reject collectivism imposed by elites of any sort upon the working people, but allow for people at the base to take over decisions that affect their lives—that is what Marxism is all about."

Which is of course a lie, as socialism is all about imposing top-down control over the economy and the culture of a society. Indeed, so-called "bottom-up" collectivism simply means countless platoons of community organizers singing the same song in different voices.

Kurtz's research into the 1983 Socialist Scholars Conference finds advocacy for all kinds of things which would later come to fruition, some key ones under Obama. There is, for example, the exhortation by a presenter named Peter Dreier, later a major player in ACORN, for "creat[ing] government programs that only seem to be 'reforms' of the capitalist system," but in fact "are so incompatible with capitalism that they gradually precipitate the system's collapse."

In February 2012, in what would be one of the last public appearances of his life, conservative provocateur and media impresario Andrew Breitbart took to the stage at the Conservative Political Action Conference, saying he had footage that proved Obama had been all in on Critical Race Theory going back to his law school days. The footage, long hidden away in an online PBS archive, showed the young Obama giving a speech vigorously defending Harvard Law Professor Derrick Bell, the chief promoter of that then-obscure doctrine.

Bell was a highly controversial figure. A racialist to the core, he'd written not only several works on CRT, but a hyper-racist science fiction novel wherein aliens land on Earth and offer humanity a panoply of wonders in exchange for all the black people, who are of course superior to the whites.

At Harvard Bell had been engaged in a bitter fight with the school's administration – at the time still more interested in merit than diversity – over the lack of black faculty at the Law School, at one point staging a five day one-man sit-in in his own office on behalf of a pair of pro-CRT professors denied tenure based on their scholarship.

While fellow professors at the school issued a statement denouncing him as "a media manipulator who unfairly attacked the school," he enjoyed considerable support among the students, very much including his mentee Barack Obama.

Little known or understood as CRT remained in 2012, the media was quick to denounce Breitbart as a racist for revealing President Obama's early support of the doctrine and Bell, as its academic godfather. *The Atlantic* declared it more evidence of "just how intellectually bankrupt a movement conservatism has become." For its part, *Rolling Stone* tried to mainstream CRT (without revealing its toxic anti-white essence), arguing that "Anyone who thinks power and race don't figure in how the law is applied or that racism is a thing of the past is not paying attention." Chimed in *Slate's* Will Oremus, "it is part of the mainstream debates over affirmative action, immigration, and hate-crime laws."

Of course, CRT isn't obscure anymore, it's everywhere, from K-12 education, where the historically illiterate nonsense that the Revolutionary War was fought to protect slavery and racism is almost universally embraced, through corporate training, with its struggle sections aimed at making anyone with the misfortune to have been born white to be ever alert to his own innate racism.

And no one is more responsible than Derrick Bell's old pupil, Barack Obama.

Indeed, he and his people are *still* fighting to hide the truth about what CRT is and the enormous damage it inflicts.

When Florida's Ron DeSantis dared in 2023 to sign a law – one overwhelmingly supported by parents – that banned CRT indoctrination in public schools, who was the first to unload on him? Obama loyalist Arne Duncan, who as his Education Secretary had been the administration's point man in promulgating the indoctrination in the first place. Inevitably, he raged against DeSantis as – what else? – a racist. The Florida governor had a "white nationalist agenda," he claimed, and "always attacks the most vulnerable, whether it's the AP African American history, whether it's the LGBTQ community, whether it's immigrants, he always attacks the most vulnerable."

Having succeeded in turning CRT from an obscure academic theory to a cultural, political and economic aggression afflicting the entire country – and, more than that, having in the process seized the moral high ground – Obama's hatchet man could only sputter in rage and disbelief that anyone dared to fight back.

CHAPTER 9

THE BAIT AND SWITCH

The very moment Barack Obama took office, the soothing tones of the campaign rhetoric, the placating centrism of his speeches, the hagiographic portrayal as America's healer...all of it went away.

It started with his inaugural address. Traditionally, a new president takes pains to offer olive branches to the party out of power, and at least pretend to care about how important it is to come together for the common good.

That wasn't Obama. His speech, widely lauded as "historic," trashed Republicans and was an outright paean to collectivism.

Quoting one of the most important lines ever written – the Declaration of Independence's "We hold these truths to be self-evident, that all men are created equal, that they are endowed by their Creator with certain unalienable Rights, that among these are Life, Liberty and the pursuit of Happiness" – he proceeded to claim the Founders intended them to support *his* agenda. As he put it, "fidelity to our founding principles requires new responses to new challenges; that preserving our individual freedom *ultimately requires collective action."* As one critic observed, Obama was in fact "arguing counter to the Founding Fathers that the pursuit of happiness is the pursuit of equality of results, not the equality of opportunity, and that he will do what he can to use government to make everybody more equal in terms of their income and life work."

Ron Fournier of the *National Journal* was among those dismayed by the address. "What happened to the idealistic young politician who argued against dividing the country into red and blue Americas?" he wondered.

Among Obama's first *acts* as president was to order removed from the Oval Office a bust of Winston Churchill – as brazen a symbolic repudiation as could be imagined not just of the great wartime leader, but of the muscular Western tradition he so ably represented.

Of course, both at home and across the Atlantic, the media rose to Obama's defense. As CNN blandly observed, the removal was merely part of an "Oval Office redesign" featuring "new busts instead: Latino civil rights leader Cesar Chavez, Rev. Martin Luther King Jr., Robert F. Kennedy, Rosa Parks and Eleanor Roosevelt."

While more discerning observers interpreted the bust's removal as an act of filial devotion to Barack Obama, Sr.'s anti-colonialism, it is likely at least as much the product of the unceasing tirades against the entire Anglo-American post-war project that the young Obama absorbed at the feet of his ideological father, Frank Marshall Davis.

Too, almost immediately, Obama brought forth the American Recovery and Reinvestment Act of 2009. This "stimulus" bill passed the House on January 28, 2009, by a partisan 244–188 vote, and the Senate two weeks later by a 61–37 margin. While ARRA was advertised as spending its $800 billion on "infrastructure," the definition of the term expanded faster than Lizzo at a Whataburger.

What did the American economy get out of ARRA? In the words of famous NFL coach Jim Mora, diddly poo.

Take, as an example, rural broadband internet, hailed by Obama as not just an economic necessity but, crucially, as a social-justice one as well. But, as economists Jeffrey Eisenach and Kevin Caves concluded in a research paper published two years later, the costs involved were nothing short of insane. How crazy? Try $349,234. Per home. Which was more than twice the value of the average home in the areas involved.

Clearly, Obama wasn't the first president (and hardly the first Democrat) who thought the best way to stimulate the economy was to throw money out of helicopters at an unsuspecting public. Ever since the appearance on the scene of the leftist god of economics, John Maynard Keynes, this had pretty much been progressive economic gospel. But in justification of his own policies, Obama would take it a decisive ideological step further. As his "You Didn't Build That" doctrine later had it, government action was the key element in fostering economic success. Hard work and individual initiative were secondary.

Yet Obama's runaway government spending quickly led not to growth, but economic stagnation, flattening out what would otherwise have been a sharp economic rebound from the economic crash of 2007 and 2008.

Nor was ARRA by any means the only bit of domestic policy abuse the new president had to offer. Another of the disastrous early bills passed by his commanding majorities in the House and Senate was the Lilly Ledbetter Fair Pay Act of 2009, which relaxed the statute of limitations for equal-pay lawsuits. An overreaction to a May 2007 Supreme Court decision, *Ledbetter v. Goodyear Tire & Rubber Co.*, the bill shifted the balance dramatically against employers by effectively eliminating time limits for filing all manner of discrimination claims related to pay, even as it did nothing to resolve the supposed problem of equal pay for women. What it did do was offer up a smorgasbord of opportunities for plaintiff attorneys to gin up clients.

Then there was the expanded State Children's Health Insurance Program (S-CHIP), which led to a mountain of abuse and perverse incentives and served as a precursor to the Obamacare Medicaid expansion.

And there was the shutting down of the Keystone XL pipeline, which was a major attack on domestic – that is, North American – energy production.

And all kinds of other intrusive federal policies that amounted to attacks on the free market.

And the auto bailouts.

In the wake of the economic shock of the 2008 recession, America's Big Three automakers were all suffering badly from a collapse in consumer demand, and only one, Ford, was in a good position to survive the downturn.

Obama decided he'd use Troubled Asset Relief Program (TARP) to bail out all of the Big Three. To the tune of $80 billion.

The result was near-nationalization of the auto industry, with General Motors – in Frank Marshall Davis's writings, the single greatest of all corporate bogeymen – at its center. In a 1950 *Honolulu Record* column, for instance, Davis decried the fact that the previous year the company had garnered more profit than any other corporation in history. "Obviously, a business that can show a profit in one year of $600,000,000 is in a position to control government..." he raged. "And so, with still rising unemployment and a mounting depression, the time draws nearer when we will have to decide to oust the monopolies and restore a competing system of free enterprise, or let the government own and operate our major industries."

And now Barack Obama had done just that, capturing the company for government, and turning it into a government zombie.

To this day, he touts the auto bailouts as a great success.

There are two different issues with the bailouts. Libertarians have argued against the government rescue of the big banks and the automakers as setting a terrible precedent. "By going in to bail out companies — not the industry, we were bailing out a couple of companies that had made bad decisions — we were shielding them from the effects of their decisions," observes economist Daniel Ikenson of the Cato Institute. The alternative, they point out, would have been temporary pain and dislocation, but an ultimately stronger industry and economy. (Though "saved," General Motors is now more aptly described as Government Motors.)

But there is an even more disturbing aspect to the bailout. The Obama administration decided to reduce the amounts owed to General Motors and Chrysler bondholders without the approval of Congress or through negotiations with these creditors. As many people noted at the time, this "haircut" was a violation of the clause in the Fifth Amendment which says that people cannot be deprived of their property without just compensation and due process of law. This was an unprecedented act. Never before in history had a President unilaterally and illegally taken property from American citizens on such a scale.

Needless to say, the legacy media swooned over the massive government infringement on the economy and on fundamental constitutional rights. "We Are All Socialists Now," declared the cover of *Newsweek* in February 2009.

Written by Jon Meacham, the story inside giddily predicted that "(W)hether we want to admit it or not—and many, especially Congressman Pence and Hannity, do not— the America of 2009 is moving toward a modern European state."

The comparisons to FDR and the New Deal were ubiquitous – on *CNN, NPR, CBS, NBC, The New York Times, The Los Angeles Times,* and *The Washington Post* – and the new president ate them up.

"I would put these first four months up against any prior administration since FDR," he crowed in May. "We didn't ask for the challenges that we face, but we don't shrink from them either."

As for his critics, he dismissed them out of hand. "What's happened is that whenever a president tries to bring about significant changes, particularly during times of economic unease, then there is a certain segment of the population that gets very riled up. FDR was called a socialist and a communist."

But in contrast to Obama, Roosevelt had run on a program of "bold, persistent experimentation" with economic policy as a means of escaping the Great Depression. Voters had more or less known what to expect.

Obama was all bait and switch. Aside from the relative handful who'd paid close attention to his background, few had much warning of what was coming. Now that it was here and doing great damage to the economy and their own futures, many were experiencing massive shock.

The result? The Tea Party movement was born on February 9, 2009, less than a month into Obama's presidency on, of all places, CNBC.

Rick Santelli, a heretofore unknown reporter working the floor of the Chicago Board of Trade for CNBC, suddenly erupted in a diatribe against the new president's radical restructuring of the American economy that had the auto companies and large financial institutions, among others, getting massive infusions of fiat cash, with copious strings attached. Santelli was particularly appalled by Obama's newly announced housing bailout plan, advertised as a means to help some homeowners refinance mortgages and avoid foreclosure. It was a flat betrayal of the America Santelli had grown up in and its creed of success born of discipline and personal responsibility, and he just couldn't take it anymore.

"Government is promoting bad behavior!" he proclaimed on live TV. ". . . Do we really want to subsidize the losers' mortgages? This is America! How many of you people want to pay for your neighbor's mortgage? President Obama, are you listening? How about we all stop paying our mortgages! It's a moral hazard."

Harkening back to revolutionary times, Santelli spontaneously called for a latter-day Tea Party in protest of the government's bailout orgy.

In almost no time, a nationwide movement was born. It manifested itself in remarkably well-attended rallies across the country and spawned hundreds of advocacy groups plying their trade at the local, state and national level. The Tea Party generated so much passion that it would be credited with the following year's massive off-year wave election for the Republicans.

The movement was organic, unorganized and diverse, but it was loud. Americans saw what Obama was doing and did not like it one bit.

But Obama was having none of it.

Breathlessly, the *New York Times'* leftist blogger Charles Lemos summed up what instantly became a standard liberal narrative. After watching the Santelli clip, he wrote "I first had to check my calendar. Somehow, I felt I traveled back in time to the early 1970s to witness first hand Richard Nixon's 'northern strategy,' his pursuit of white ethnic voters who were so deeply disaffected over Great Society programs ranging from desegregation (remember the Boston busing madness?) to affirmative action among others that they would desert the Democratic Party, becoming 'Nixon's silent majority' and 'Reagan Democrats'.

". . .Rick Santelli is heir to this legacy laced with racist overtones. Note the promo before the rant in the video link at CNBC. CNBC has an upcoming special entitled The Rise of America's New Black Overclass. Fear mongering, it's worked before so let's try it again. It's back to the 1970s for the GOP and their rabid white ethnics."

Lemos added that he had spent a decade on Wall Street and found there "a largely liberal environment with one major exception, the trading floor. In my experience I found traders, who are largely white ethnics — Irish, Italian, Greek, Polish or Slovak among others — and graduates of the Seton Halls, the Boston Colleges, the Notre Dames, the Penn States were the most rabid conservative and foul-mouthed people on the planet."

Of course. It had to be racism, not principle, which underlay Santelli's criticism. Who but a racist would object to Obama's bailouts? And object to bailing out disproportionately African-American homeowners behind on their mortgages and facing foreclosure, well…that's the very definition of bigotry, isn't it?

Thus began what in mainstream circles would be the reflex to define all criticism of Obama or his policies as not only ill-informed, but vile. Any suggestion of return to old-fashioned market economics in America was now to be treated by Barack Obama and his sycophants as a racist dog-whistle.

And even with Obama gone as the party's public face, it has never stopped. The same venomous opprobrium is heaped by Joe Biden's Obama Redux administration, often by the loathsome Biden himself, on everyone from critics of COVID lockdowns to those objecting to trans "women" competing in sports.

It wasn't supposed to go this way, not in a democracy.

And that wasn't even the worst of it. That would be the outright war on conservatives declared by Obama's Department of Homeland Security in a nine-page memo on April

7, 2009. This was eight days before the scheduled nationwide April 15 Tax Day Tea Party protests. Entitled "Right-wing Extremism: Current Economic and Political Climate Fueling Resurgence in Radicalization and Recruitment," it characterized even the most common modes of conservative expression, from anti-abortion protests to Second Amendment rights activism, to organizing for border security, as seedbeds of "white supremacy." It warned that "the historical election of an African American president and the prospect of policy changes are proving to be a driving force for rightwing extremist recruitment and radicalization… Rightwing extremists are harnessing this historical election as a recruitment tool. Many rightwing extremists are antagonistic toward the new presidential administration and its perceived stance on a range of issues, including immigration and citizenship, the expansion of social programs to minorities, and restrictions on firearms as well as white supremacists' longstanding exploitation of social issues such as abortion, inter-racial crimes, and same-sex marriage."

The document concludes with a call for others "to report information concerning suspicious or criminal activity to DHS and the FBI."

In short, if you opposed Barack Obama and his radical, Marxist agenda, you were a white supremacist. Sound familiar?

CHAPTER 10

OBAMA'S ENEMIES LIST: HALF OF AMERICA

Homeland Security's 2009 "Right-wing extremism" memo was not only a chilling insight into the administration's mentality. It was the beginning of the weaponization of the federal government against its own citizens.

Before he was done, Obama would impose his Hard Left values on his party, and tutor supporters in his toxic scorched-earth politics, making it a matter of faith among Democrats that their millions of fellow citizens on the other side were not merely mistaken in their views, but fundamentally indecent. They were not just lacking in basic humanity and compassion, but racist.

Only yesterday, during the just-concluded Bush Administration, liberals had cast dissent as patriotic. Now, under Obama, it was redefined as dangerous, with the behavior (and even the speech) of those who challenged the regime needing to be closely monitored and, when necessary, criminalized.

Indeed, inept as Team Obama was in other respects, when it came to suppressing perceived threats they were ruthlessly, brutally efficient.

Always behind the smiling façade of hope and change.

In August 2009, four months after the Homeland Security memo, a blog post on the official White House web site went a step further. It urged Americans to report on the "scary chain emails and videos," "rumors," "emails," and even "casual conversation" of their fellow citizens. For convenience's sake, the invitation to turn Stasi on one's fellow man included a contact form linked to a dedicated White House email address.

Unsurprisingly, the "snitch line" generated a good bit of controversy.

But even that was nothing compared to what was coming.

Operation Fast and Furious is recalled, by most who remember it at all, as one of those minor affairs ginned up by the political opposition that was quickly exposed as amounting to not very much. This just shows how effective Team Obama and their media allies were in suppressing the truth. In fact, Fast and Furious might well be the most underreported-on government scandal in American history.

It is surely among the most egregious examples of (literal) government weaponization.

What was Fast and Furious? Essentially, the Bureau of Alcohol, Tobacco, Firearms, and Explosives (ATF) greased the wheels for purchases of guns in the United States by straw purchasers, to be walked over the border and put into the hands of Mexican drug cartels. Ostensibly, its purpose was to facilitate prosecutions of cartel members on weapons charges.

But as so often with Team Obama's machinations, there was malicious method behind the seeming madness.

Launched in 2009, Fast and Furious moved a couple of thousand firearms from the U.S. to Mexico. These included AR-15s and Kalashnikovs. Most disappeared into the ether. Until, that is, they began showing back up in ways that weren't good.

Mexican civilians died in staggering numbers. We don't even have close to a full count of the number, and innocent people are still being caught in the crossfire from the Fast and Furious guns used in the cartel wars.

Of particular interest to Americans were the pair of law enforcement agents stationed at the border, Border Patrol agent Brian Terry and Immigration and Customs Enforcement (ICE) agent Jaime Zapata, who were shot and killed with guns connected to Fast and Furious.

So was this merely a bumbling disaster of a sting operation aimed at bringing down the cartels, as the media claimed?

To the contrary, considerable evidence indicates it had a very different goal: to cast American gun-sellers as responsible for the carnage across the border, thus building a case for anti-gun measures that would otherwise not pass Congress. In short, it was intended as a means to short-circuit the Second Amendment.

The evidence came in December 2011, when then-CBS News reporter Sharyl Attkisson obtained documents showing the intent of ATF officials was to buttress the case for Obama's gun control agenda.

Under other circumstances, such a revelation would have been explosive, provoking a scandal big enough to take down an administration.

But not this time. Not under this president.

What followed were years of deceit, stonewalling and denial.

Obama claimed straight-face that he'd only just heard of the operation "on the news" and that he was furious about it. His wingman, Attorney General Eric Holder, the official directly responsible for the operation, who should have been fired on the spot, lied even more brazenly that it was also news to him. "I probably heard about Fast and Furious for the first time over the last few weeks," as Holder baldly asserted in May 2011. In fact, Attkisson later established that Holder had known about Fast and Furious by July 2010, if not earlier.

When it became clear that Attkisson, a rare unbought mainstream journalist, was going to continue to dig, the administration put the screws on CBS to shut her up. "I'm also calling Sharyl's editor and reaching out to (Bob) Schieffer," wrote Holder's top press aide, Tracy Schmaler, in a panicked email to White House Deputy Press Secretary Eric Schultz. "She's out of control."

The brazen stonewalling – including the withholding of key documents – went on throughout hearings of the Republican-led House Judiciary Committee, and in its frustration, the full House eventually voted Attorney General Holder in both civil and criminal contempt of Congress, a first in American history.

But, in vivid contrast to later persecutions of Republicans for far more trivial offenses, nothing came of it.

In fact, in its extraordinary above-the-law arrogance, Team Obama had House Democrats conduct their own Potemkin Fast and Furious investigation. "Contrary to repeated claims by some," Rep. Elijah E. Cummings (D-MD) duly summed up the minority report's hastily-contrived "findings", "the committee has obtained no evidence that Operation Fast and Furious was a politically motivated operation conceived and directed by high-level Obama administration political appointees at the Department of Justice."

The Congressional Black Caucus, for its part, accused the Republican majority of…wait for it…racism.

Successful as the cover-up was, Fast and Furious itself had failed abysmally in its intended purpose of smearing the pro-gun community. But Obama had other enemies, and other scores to settle, and was just as ready to go to extraordinary lengths to settle them. And at the very top of the list was the Tea Party, which had played such a key role in the shellacking of the Dems (and the repudiation of the Obama agenda) in the 2010 midterms. Obama himself had reportedly been caught short by the electoral slam-down, and expecting a tight reelection race in 2012, he was going to make damned sure it wouldn't happen again.

So next he turned to the IRS.

As everyone who cares to know does, his IRS point person in the plot to strangle in its crib the burgeoning network of conservative 501(c)(4) organizations comprising the Tea Party was one Lois Lerner, the agency's Director of Exempt Organizations, the key decision maker on what organizations received tax exempt status. Operating with an audacity that Richard Nixon could only have dreamed of, Lerner scarcely even bothered to be discrete. In a video from a 2010 appearance at Duke University, she openly admitted that Team Obama had tasked her agency with shutting down the troublesome grassroots conservative groups in advance of the 2012 election.

"Everyone is up in arms because they don't like it," she said of the money flowing from corporations to 501(c)(4) groups. "Federal Election Commission can't do anything about it; they want the IRS to fix the problem…So everybody is screaming at us right now 'Fix it now before the election. Can't you see how much these people are spending?'"

And did the weaponization of the IRS ever work! Before it was over, Lerner and her division wouldn't just target those

Tea Party-affiliated groups to strip them of their tax-free status. In what the *National Review's* Eliana Johnson termed "likely the largest unauthorized disclosure of tax-return information in history," the IRS took the extraordinary further step of sending more than a million pages of tax returns to the Justice Department.

Moreover, Lerner sent Holder's DOJ a mountain of IRS Schedule B data, including the names and addresses of contributors to those conservative groups. This was an unprecedented document dump. Anyone who gave to a Tea Party organization in that time period effectively went on an Obama administration enemies list.

How high up did the IRS scandal go? Lerner herself let slip that it went all the way to the White House. Little wonder that eventually, late on a Friday afternoon to minimize coverage, it was "announced" that the IRS had lost 28 months' worth of Lois Lerner's emails... after a year of "looking."

So, the GOP Senate found itself out of luck in looking for proof of what Obama knew and when he knew it.

The president, for his part, interviewed by Fox News' Bill O'Reilly before the 2012 Super Bowl, was as confidently arrogant as ever, breezily maintaining there wasn't a "smidgeon" of corruption involved in the IRS scandal. And in the end, nothing happened to Lerner, or then-IRS commissioner John Koskinen, or anyone else.

But the Tea Party – which might have coalesced into a coalition capable of promoting long-term conservative electoral success, as have the coalitions of the hard left in their takeover of the Democrat Party – was finished as a political movement.

However, this was not the end of Obama's weaponization of the federal government. In the run-up to his reelection campaign against the hapless Mitt Romney, Obama would go on to create a fact-checking microsite to identify and vilify prominent donors to his rival's campaign, dumping their names on Twitter and blasting them out in emails to supporters. Las Vegas casino magnate Sheldon Adelson, for one, was smeared as a crook. This was the excuse Eric Holder needed to launch an investigation into Adelson's Las Vegas Sands Corporation for supposed money laundering. Similar intimidation tactics targeted the Koch brothers and others. The message: If the Supreme Court was going to hold that political donations were free speech, as it had in the recent *Citizens United* decision so loathed by the left, GOP political donors should expect to get roughed up, and then some.

Hardly by chance, for Obama and his congressional allies, the demise of the Tea Party coincided nicely with the bludgeoning through Congress of his signature program, Obamacare.

Yet even with its activist shock troops sidelined, Republican opposition to the plan remained united and strong, thanks to widespread recognition that a bill aimed at wholly remaking American healthcare was a flat-out assault on free enterprise, one that harbored vast unforeseen consequences for both the economy and the rhythms of daily life. Long before it was to come to a vote, tens of millions of ordinary Americans knew that Obama's famous declaration – "If you like your doctor, you will be able to keep your doctor. Period. If you like your health-care plan, you will be able to keep your health-care plan. Period. No one will take it away. No matter what." – had been a shameless lie. As even the non-partisan Congressional Budget Office had it, passage of the measure meant "seven million fewer people will have employment-based health insurance."

Yet as far as Obama and Democrats were concerned, the GOP stance had less to do with philosophy than with... racism.

As Mississippi congressman Bennie Thompson asserted, it was "just because a black man created it."

In Senate debate, West Virginia's Jay Rockefeller echoed that view, declaring "it's just we don't want anything good to happen under this president, because he's the wrong color." For her part, Louisiana state senator and state Democratic Party head Karen Carter Peterson waved away even that mild qualifier. "You want to know what it's about?" she demanded of her colleagues. "It's about race. Now nobody wants to talk about that. It's about the race of this African-American president. . . . It comes down to the race of the president of the U.S., which causes people to disconnect and step away from the substance of the bill."

The media naturally ran with that dubious narrative. As the *Washington Post* had it, in a piece entitled "Yes, opposition to Obamacare is tied up with race," "conservatives have been told for years that the law is an act of racial vengeance."

Lunacy though it was, for most mainstream Democrats, this no longer registered as hyperbole. Under Obama it is what they had by now come to believe. Amid the Obamacare fight, even left-of-center columnist Jonathan Chait conceded that "Liberals dwell in a world of paranoia of a white racism that has seeped out of American history in the Obama years and lurks everywhere, mostly undetectable." Conservatives," he added, "believe 'racism' is used as a cudgel to delegitimize their core beliefs."

True enough, Chait characterized this last as their own form of paranoia. But of course, he'd never been on the receiving end. As Obama himself is so fond of saying, he and his stand on "the right side of history," while his opponents are on the "wrong side."

Yet this may not be the most important part of the story regarding Obamacare. If Fast and Furious was the most underreported government scandal of recent decades, the failure of Obamacare to improve U.S. health care is surely the most underreported fact. Voters were repeatedly told that Obamacare would reduce healthcare costs even though every worker in the country had to pay a new tax as did employers and the wealthy alike. As the Supreme Court noted in justifying the constitutionality of this massive increase in federal power: it was the largest tax increase in American history. But, it was said, it would save lives, as once it was implemented health outcomes would dramatically improve.

In fact, the opposite happened. Throughout the post-war era, the U.S. mortality rate persistently declined. For example, it was 1,155 deaths per 100,000 people in 1937, but by 1986 that had fallen to 876.7. It reached an all-time low of 794.5 when Obama was elected. It has never been so low since. This increase in the death rate came long before the Covid pandemic, and it tracks closely with the introduction of Obamacare.

And there is good reason to think that the two are related. Obamacare increased the number of Americans with health insurance. The main way it did this was by boosting the count of those previously uninsured with Medicaid. Yet as everyone in the business of studying healthcare knew – including those who wrote the Obamacare bill – patients with Medicaid don't have better health care than those without it. In fact, a study by the University of Virgina concluded that your likelihood of dying if you face major surgery is greater with Medicaid than with no insurance. That's because the most capable surgeons don't take Medicaid, but all hospitals are required by law to provide treatment to ill patients even if they don't have insurance. Thus, a patient with Medicaid is likely to get a worse heart or brain surgeon than one who has no insurance. Obamacare has given work to many of our least competent doctors, and it has given less employment to our best.

It also threw money at many small and rural health care clinics. These were often the "pill-mills" that drove the opioid crisis. That was happening as the Obama foreign policy agenda of appeasing China and weakening the border with Mexico led to that flood into our towns and cities of fentanyl and crystal meth.

All this raises the question of what the actual purpose of the Affordable Health Care Act really was. The media did occasionally report on this: by the open admission of many Democrats in Congress, it was simply a step towards their larger goal of socialized medicine.

As this goal of fundamentally transforming America involves such high stakes, it provided reason for demonizing its enemies. And over and over, Obama made clear his resentments were not only political but personal, and that they ran very deep. He and his supporters represented justice, while those who opposed him stood for bigotry and hatred.

He set the tone, and the marching orders were out – this was blood sport, and anyone opposing the left agenda was fair game. There could be no live-and-let-live in Barack Obama's America.

This was never more evident than in the administration's attacks on communities of belief in the wake of Obamacare's passage, as the measure was swiftly weaponized against Obama's cultural and political enemies.

In probably the most shocking instance of the administration's bullying, they went after even the Little Sisters of the Poor, Catholic nuns who have provided hospice care to the elderly poor and dying for nearly two centuries, demanding the Catholic organization provide birth control pills as part of the new law's federally-mandated health insurance policy. For the Little Sisters, caving to the federal bullies on their most deeply held (and heretofore protected) beliefs was obviously no choice at all, and they were forced to go to court. It would take seven years before they were finally vindicated by the Supreme Court.

As Dennis Prager observes, "Every time you think that the left and its political party have hit moral bottom, they will eventually prove you wrong."

Nonetheless, Barack Obama is the moral model for today's Democrats.

When was the turning point? Hard to say with precision, but there were definite markers along the way, and the Little Sisters slap-down was certainly one.

Another was the 2014 case of Brendan Eich, the co-founder of internet browser company Mozilla, who'd recently been named the company's CEO. A devout Christian, six years earlier Eich had written a check for a thousand dollars to support passage of a constitutional amendment in California to ban gay marriage. At the time, this was a position that Obama himself still supported, as did most Democrats. The proposition passed going away, with wide support from, among others, black and Hispanic Democratic voters.

But six years later, with the cultural tides in flux, the left went after Eich for that donation in both social media and the mainstream press. So powerful was the assault, that – in a harrowing preview of the cancel culture to come – he was forced to resign nine days after his appointment as CEO.

True, Obama had no direct connection with the episode. But having by then spent six years engaging in brass-knuckled intimidation, he didn't have to. Once that pump had been primed, the cultural pressure on traditional America had changed from a trickle to a gusher.

CHAPTER 11

APOLOGIZING FOR GREATNESS

In key respects, Obama's foreign policy was philosophically akin to that behind the auto bailouts. It, too, was rooted in his abiding contempt for an America rooted in traditional values and epoch changing achievements.

Yes, America had taken its foreign policy lumps in recent decades – most obviously in the Bush era's tragically ill-advised Mideast wars and efforts at nation-building that had exacted such a price in blood, treasure, and national self-confidence. For that, full accountability has proven elusive.

But for all that, in 2008 we remained unchallenged as the greatest nation on earth. We had long been, and remained, the beacon of hope and most cherished destination of people everywhere around the globe. The nation that had, more than once in the previous century, reluctantly sent its sons off to help save the world from totalitarianism. Indeed, this had been the noble impulse behind the recent misadventures.

We were a *good* nation.

Furthermore, not only did our system of free market capitalism serve us well, but it enriched the entire world beyond imagination, dramatically reducing poverty and hunger while increasing opportunity.

Millions of Americans grew up taking this for granted – and taking in it great and understandable pride.

But not Barack Obama. From the start, his view was that of his mentors: that America was hubristic and oppressive, the world's bully.

And now, in the nation's highest office, remedying it was a key aspect of the "fundamental transformation" he aimed to bring about.

His chief advisor in this respect was the smug and overbearingly self-righteous Samantha Power, whose 2002 book *A Problem from Hell: America and the Age of Genocide* had made her a darling of liberal intelligentsia. Power had been a member of his 2008 campaign team before she briefly made herself politically toxic for trashing Hillary Clinton as a "monster." But she was right back in the fold by the transition, ending up on the National Security Council.

An Irish immigrant to the U.S., Power inspired what first conservatives and then much of the rest of America were soon derisively terming Obama's "Apology Tour." In 2003, she'd written an article in *The New Republic* explicitly demanding precisely the disgraceful, self-flagellating globe-trotting the new president was so happy to undertake.

American foreign policy, she declared in the piece, "needs not tweaking but overhauling. We need: a historical reckoning with crimes committed, sponsored, or permitted by the United States... A country has to look back before it can move forward..."

Noting that former German chancellor Willy Brant had gone down on one knee in the Warsaw ghetto, and that that gesture had been ennobling and cathartic for Germany, she asked "would such an approach be futile for the United States?"

Yes, she equated U.S. foreign policy with the crimes of Nazi Germany.

Reagan-era UN Ambassador Jean Kirkpatrick, whose job Power ultimately held in Obama's second term, had long had Power's number as a naïve fool, branding her and her ilk the "Blame America First" crowd.

But now her gibberish was the basis of American foreign policy, as soon after the inauguration Obama took to the skies to travel the globe, trashing America at every stop. The groveling *mea culpas* came everywhere from Western Europe to Latin America, to (most especially), the Muslim world, for America's sins past and present, exaggerated and imagined, the rhetoric referencing the nation's lofty theoretical principles even as it took the Marxist view of our consistent failure to uphold them.

"The United States is still working through some of our own darker periods in our history," as he declared in Ankara, Turkey in April, 2009. "Facing the Washington Monument that I spoke of is a memorial of Abraham Lincoln, the man who freed those who were enslaved even after Washington led our Revolution. Our country still struggles with the legacies of slavery and segregation..."

This before the Turks, among the most genocidal nations in world history.

On and on it went, country after country.

In 2011, it was revealed by Wikileaks that Obama had planned to travel to Japan in September 2009 to apologize for Hiroshima and Nagasaki – presumably, without any mention of Pearl Harbor – until the Japanese government vetoed that trip. No matter: seven years later, eight months before the end of his term, Obama did make it to Hiroshima and delivered that apology.

Clearly, he had taken to heart the lessons learned, at Frank Marshall Davis's knee, as well as those picked up in Edward Said's Columbia classes, or hanging out with Rashid Khalidi at the University of Chicago, and the many imparted during twenty years in Jeremiah Wright's "Goddamn America" church.

Anti-Americanism was the logical foreign policy of an anti-American.

Still, for all the many Americans for whom this came as a shock, there were others who'd had his number all along. In an October 2009 column, conservative pundit Charles Krauthammer posited that Obama wanted to reduce America's role in the world not only because he believed the nation lacked the moral capacity to be a superpower, but so that the savings could be invested in the expanding welfare state, with the ultimate aim of turning the U.S. into a larger version of the Western European social democracies, with their pitifully weak militaries and cradle-to-grave nanny states.

As if in confirmation, that very month the Sweden-based Nobel committee awarded Obama the Nobel Peace Prize.

At the time, the award inspired a mix of incredulity and mockery, since Obama had been in office less than a year and had achieved nothing. But today, with eight years in office recalled as a time of little peace and even less meaningful effort toward that end, it is widely recognized as a low point in the Nobel organization's history. Indeed, what Obama *would* convincingly evince was a wholehearted abdication of responsibility for protecting America's national security or vital economic interests.

The pattern began with his response to the jihadist terrorist attack at Ft. Hood , Texas that occurred just a couple of weeks after the Nobel committee paid off the Apology Tour with its hardware.

"Allahu Akbar," screamed the terrorist Nidal Malik Hasan, before opening fire and slaughtering 13 defenseless American soldiers at the base's medical processing facility on November 5.

It was the first time in 230 years of American history that a commissioned officer in the U.S. military turned his weapons against fellow soldiers in a committed attack, and it clearly represented a shift that was as ominous as it was tragic. It proved that the political correctness, multiculturalism and the victimization fetishes that were increasingly prevalent in America weren't just noxious; they were deadly.

Moreover, in this case what happened should have been foreseen. Hasan – an American military officer – had been traveling around Killeen, Texas in fundamentalist Muslim garb giving away Korans. Earlier, he had been a regular at Great Falls, Virginia's Dar al-Hijrah mosque, whose imam was a jihadist banned in Britain for his support of terror, and whose fellow congregants included Nawaf al-Hamzi and Hani Hanjour, soon thereafter two of the four hijackers of American Airlines Flight 77, piloted into the Pentagon on September 11.

So warning signs were everywhere. Hasan was on the radar. The very day of his attack, he scrawled out Islamic verses on his door. Yet no one stopped him, for fear of being called an Islamaphobe.

By the time Obama took office it had long been obvious that our enemy in the War on Terror was promoting a fifth column within our military. The Obama administration refused to see a problem.

Following the Fort Hood massacre, it hurried to apologize – only not to the victims. Homeland Security director Janet Napolitano declared that her priority was to insure there would be no "backlash" against Muslims. Astonishingly, the attack itself was attributed to "workplace violence."

Moreover, Napolitano took the opportunity to emphasize that the real danger to American security came from "right-wing terrorists," especially ex-military types.

The narrative had been established by Homeland Security's "Right-wing extremism" memo soon after Obama took office, and it has never changed. As we know, a decade and a half later, on exactly those grounds, the Obamaites running things under putative president Joe Biden would weaponize the FBI against public school parents seeking redress for the maltreatment of their children.

Hence, up and down the chain, Obama underlings knew to dutifully spout the same inanities. "Our diversity, not only in our Army, but in our country, is a strength," Army Gen. George Casey, offering the country his dose of it's-a-small-world bilge. "And as horrific as this tragedy was, if our diversity becomes a casualty, I think that's worse."

Indeed, in the Ft. Hood massacre, the lives of our servicemen were openly subsumed to the principles of what would come to be called Diversity, Equity and Inclusion.

And next it was the shooting of a Department of Public Health Christmas Party in San Bernardino, CA by Syed Rizwan Farook and Tashfeen Malik, killing 14 and injuring 22. Neighbors of Farook and Malik observed suspicious activity for months preceding the shooting but said nothing out of the fear they would be accused of "racial profiling." As commentator Mark Steyn phrased it, "see something, say nothing."

Here, indeed, were the already-sprouting seeds of America's woke military.

The Apology Tour wasn't just an overseas contingency operation. It was aimed at beating the idea of pervasive American evil into the nation's conception of itself.

Along those same lines, there was Afghanistan. It is easily forgotten that Obama came into office characterizing Afghanistan as "the good war" in contrast to the one fought simultaneously in Iraq. He said he was going to win it.

Obama trumpeted his new Afghanistan strategy at a press conference on March 27, 2009, and he changed commanding generals in the Afghan theater in order to pursue it. But once Gen. Stanley McChrystal outlined the resources he needed to do so, the president spent months "dithering and waffling," in the words of former Vice President Dick Cheney, finally giving McChrystal half the troops he'd asked for, then giving the enemy a time frame by which they could plan to lay low and avoid fighting against a U.S. troop surge by announcing a withdrawal date.

We all know how Afghanistan ended. Just as Obama offered feckless and uninterested leadership to the detriment of our troops in Afghanistan, so would his people running the Biden ship of state.

And even as he was breaking faith with our troops, Obama-style leadership also meant savaging some of our closest and most effective allies. Like, for (pointed) example, Israel.

In November 2011, Obama traveled to Cannes, France, for the G20 summit, where he had a one-on-one meeting with French premier Nicolas Sarkozy. A key moment was caught on a hot mic. The subject: Israeli prime minister Benjamin Netanyahu.

"Netanyahu!" Sarkozy exclaimed. "I can't stand him. He's a liar."

Obama's reply? "You're sick of him? I have to work with him every day."

It was no surprise, then, that a couple of years later it came out that Obama was directing American tax dollars into an effort to derail Netanyahu's re-election efforts. But not a word from the media about "election interference."

Why? Because Netanyahu got in the way of Obama's attempts to force Israel to make concessions to the Palestinians in exchange for a "peace" that anyone who knew anything about the region understood the Palestinians would never deliver.

Obama had come into office demanding that the Palestinians get an independent state of their own by the end of his first term — never mind how poorly-organized and otherwise unsustainable such a state would be. Already the Arab and Iranian money handed to the Palestinians in "aid" went not for building power or water systems, or running schools, but instead for terrorist training and rockets. Nonetheless, the demand was for Israel to make peace with an entity, or lack of one, which was solely incentivized along cultural, religious, political and economic lines for permanent war.

But, of course, for the hard left of which Obama is a part, Israel is an obsession – routinely characterized as an "oppressive," "Apartheid," or "Nazi" state. Obama had been personally tutored in the subject by Edward Said and Rashid Khalidi, and top advisor Power's babblings on the Israel-Palestinian question were wholly in line with theirs. The president should not fear to "alienate a domestic [Jewish] constituency of tremendous political and financial import," she wrote, of Jews' traditional support of Democrats. "... America's important historic relationship with Israel has often led foreign policy decision-makers to defer reflexively to Israeli security assessments, and to replicate Israeli tactics, which, as the war in Lebanon ... demonstrated, can turn out to be counter-productive."

Under Obama, such rote leftist blame-Israel cant became policy. Israel received no credit as the sole functioning democracy in a corner of the world where brutality and the vilest forms of totalitarianism are the norm, and Team Obama never seemed to bother about the fact it was always the Arabs who initiated hostilities.

In his never-ending row with Netanyahu, Obama demanded that our putative ally Israel retreat to its pre-1967 borders, while failing to demand of the Palestinians that they so much as concede Israel's right to exist.

Among the "smart power" set, this was called "responsible diplomacy," and Obama's State Department kept doubling and tripling down on stupid.

At one point, Obama dispatched Secretary of State Hillary Clinton to read Netanyahu the riot act. Among the president's demands: that Israel release a substantial number of Palestinian prisoners as a token of goodwill; that it lift its siege of Gaza; that it suspend all settlements in the West Bank and Jerusalem; that it accept that a symbolic number of Palestinians be given the "right of return" to Israel under a future peace treaty; and that the Israelis agree to place the question of the status of Jerusalem at the top of the peace-talks agenda.

"If you refuse these demands," Hillary told Netanyahu, "the United States government will conclude that we no longer share the same interests."

This was in early March of 2010. By the end of the month, Netanyahu had to come to the White House to absorb another tongue-lashing, this time directly from Obama. And when the president was finished, he went upstairs to the residence to eat dinner with his family, leaving the Israeli leader to stew in the Roosevelt Room. When Netanyahu and his party asked for victuals of their own, they were served non-kosher food which some of them couldn't eat.

A couple of weeks after this disgraceful episode Obama was giving speeches insinuating that American troops were dying in Iraq and Afghanistan because Israel refused to make peace with the Palestinians.

It was calumny with vicious intent, and it further emboldened Hamas and the other jihadist groups in their incessant attacks on Israel.

Obama's hostility toward the Jewish state and its leader was so overt and unapologetic that even some of the American Jewish groups in the Obama coalition were up in arms, and Obama was obliged to have Netanyahu back to the White House. In the photo op that followed, the president had to absorb a lecture about the Middle East and have the Prime Minister's finger wagged in his face.

But Obama's support of Israel's enemies never wavered. In the midst of the 2014 Gaza conflict, an angry Obama called Netanyahu twice in three days to complain about civilian casualties on Gaza's streets and rooftops, while failing to so much as mention the American tax dollars going to fund Hamas' rockets – this despite the fact that one of the calls was cut short when air-raid sirens went off in Tel Aviv, forcing Netanyahu to evacuate to a bomb shelter. Obama shrugged and left to play golf at Fort Belvoir.

Obama's poisonous attitude increasingly took firm root within his party – so much so that hostility toward the Jewish state is the new norm in the Democratic Party, its traditional support for Israel a relic of the past. In progressive circles today, the blatant antisemitism of Alexandria Ocasio-Cortez and Ilhan Omar is widely seen as entirely legitimate, especially among the gullible young who make up so much of the party's base. Polls on the subject are horrifying. According to Gallup, in 2001 Democrats supported Israel over the Palestinians by 51-16%. Today 49% back the Palestinians and just 38% support Israel.

Obama's leftism shaped his foreign policy every bit as much – albeit in the opposite direction – as his embrace of Cuba's totalitarian regime likely saved Cuban communism from extinction. For by the start of Obama's second term, the Castros had been just about out of options. They had no source of hard currency to continue propping up their mafia regime. All that would have been required was to wait for the collapse; and perhaps give it a push, and at long last, after more than half a century of misery, lies and bloodshed, the old guard in Havana would finally melt away.

Instead, Obama threw the Castros an economic lifeline, his liberalization of trade serving to perpetuate the regime's hold on its people.

Nor did he even have the stomach to demand that in return the Castro regime allow free local elections, or a free currency, or real economic liberalization – meaning a Cuban might be able start a business without being a member of the communist party or having some other government connection.

So American tourist dollars and money remitted back home from the Cuban community in Miami and elsewhere went to prop up the Castro regime and sustain it the way the Russians and Venezuelans had done for decades, and the Castros once again had the resources to export revolutionary communism to the rest of Latin America.

He also opened up an American embassy in Havana. When, not long afterward, personnel stationed there complained of headaches, nausea, dizziness, blurred vision and other ailments, the administration discounted the possibility that the illnesses might have been caused by hostile enemy action – charges later determined to be true. According to a 2020 National Academies of Sciences, Engineering and Medicine report the cause of Havana Syndrome was our personnel having been hit by intense radio frequency blasts.

But Obama did not want to put our new, improved relationship with the Castros at risk. He maintained the bold opening to Cuba would be a particular boon to American agriculture – and, true enough, the scarcity and deprivation which had been the hallmark of communist regimes going back to the earliest days of the Soviet Union meant that Cubans could no longer feed themselves.

But what was left unsaid was that the Castro mob themselves would be buying those agricultural commodities and distributing them to the Cuban people, making the vaunted trade liberalization little more than a racket benefitting the criminal communist elite.

Trade liberalization, Obama-style, meant literally making the regime the sales agent for American agricultural products.

And who'd provide the loans to get those American foodstuffs onto the island? The Export-Import Bank and the U.S. Department of Agriculture – meaning the U.S. was also the banker for the transaction. And, again, not a thing was demanded in return.

Then, again, that would have required a president who actually gave a damn about the Cuban people – or American national interest.

So the Cubans went from taking to the streets and hoping America would help them achieve the freedoms they desperately sought to watching Barack Obama and Raul Castro happily join in the wave at an exhibition game in Havana between the Tampa Bay Rays and the Cuban national team. When Sen. Marco Rubio called Obama the worst presidential negotiator in his lifetime, he was giving Obama too much credit. It assumed the president was actually on our side. How naïve!

Nothing in the foreign policy sphere more alarmingly raises the question of what team Obama was playing for than his support of regime change in the Middle East. In Libya, Egypt and Syria the administration enabled the replacement of moderate Islamic regimes with more radical governments, often Muslim Brotherhood affiliated.

Indeed, this was official Obama administration policy as outlined in Presidential Study Directive-11, or PSD-11. According to the Congressional testimony of Pete Hoekstra, former Chairman of the US House of Representatives Permanent Select Committee on Intelligence, PSD-11 "ordered a government-wide reassessment of prospects for political reform in the Middle East and of the Muslim Brotherhood's role in the process."

Led by Obama National Security Advisor Ben Rhodes, the PSD-11 Task Force concluded that the Muslim Brotherhood was a "viable movement" and should be supported throughout the Middle East and North Africa. In the case of Egypt, this determination resulted in the administration's support – and triumph of -- Muslim Brotherhood affiliated radical Mohammad Morsi over the more moderate, and pro-American, Abdel Fattah el-Sisi.

In Libya, meanwhile, the once rabidly anti-American but now housetrained Moammar Qaddafi was ousted, with American support, for "humanitarian reasons." With Secretary of State Hillary Clinton notoriously cackling, "we came, we saw, he died?" The result was utter chaos and instability, including the infamous attack on our embassy in Benghazi that left three Americans dead, among them Ambassador Christopher Stevens.

While the Obamaites, in the person of National Security Advisor Susan Rice, ludicrously scrambled to assign blame for the attack to a YouTube video, in fact, as documents obtained by Judicial Watch subsequently confirmed, the United States was engaged in shipping arms from Benghazi to rebels in Syria, to be used in their U.S. backed campaign to overthrow Syrian President Bashar al-Assad. The supposedly "moderate" opposition was aligned with Al Qaeda and the Islamic State of Iraq, soon to emerge as the Islamic State of Iraq and al-Sham -- better known as ISIS.

In short, what began with the repudiation of America's overwhelmingly positive role in shaping the modern world metastasized, by the time Obama was done, to outright betrayal of our allies and of the ideals for which the nation had always stood.

Now we really did have some things to apologize for.

CHAPTER 12

ECONOMIC FASCISM

The Obama administration's fiscal performance was far and away the worst of any presidency in American history – worse, even, than those of the collapsing firms it ham-handedly bailed out in early 2009. In his first year alone, Obama ran up a deficit greater than those racked up in the combined eight years of the previous Bush administration.

But the question remains: was this merely incompetence or did it also involve something more like malevolence?

For there's no question that Team Obama's management of the economy was largely driven by a hatred of the free-market itself. Gifted a stock market crash and bank panic, Obama's team responded with policies that seemed aimed at nothing less than the crippling and cooption of the financial system.

In the process, they managed to create a brand-new form of economics nobody saw coming, along the way pulling off what amounted to a bloodless revolution.

While it was in many respects Marxist, a decade and a half later it has morphed into what may be more rightly described as fascistic.

What does that mean? Benito Mussolini's regime in Italy defined fascist economics very clearly. "Fascism should more appropriately be called corporatism because it is a merger of state and corporate power," read an entry in the Encyclopedia Italiana, composed by Mussolini's ghostwriter Giovanni Gentile.

In short, a fascist economy is one where, while individuals might still own the means of production, the operation of those means is not theirs to determine, but rather directed by the state.

In May 2009, four months after his inauguration, Obama held a dinner at the White House with nine prominent left-of-center historians, including Doris Kearns Goodwin and Michael Beschloss, during which he touted his vision for a command economy managed by federal bureaucrats, along with big employers and big unions.

It hardly need to be said that under such "state capitalism," the government would be picking winners and losers.

With that in mind, it's not surprising that at first more than a few serious capitalists actually *welcomed* Obamanomics. "He makes my job easy," as one quantitative analyst at a big-money hedge fund put it at the time. "You get some free-market Republican in office, and he'll deregulate the economy and set it loose, but you've really got to do your homework trying to pick winners. It's safer with a socialist like Obama. All I have to do is read the paper and I'll know what to do, because his people will pick all the winners for me."

What he and few others fully grasped was the insidious form this new regulatory state would take; the degree it would become an all-out assault on the private sector; or that it would lead to the consolidation of the private economy into fewer and fewer hands.

The evil genius of Obamunism was in creating fascist economics by other means.

While Obama liked to claim he saved the U.S. economy, in fact he enervated it. Labor participation plummeted; during his time in office, the American standard of living sank, and business startups evaporated, declining to chilling levels.

It was the disaster of the 2008 crash that gave Team Obama the chance to gamble on such far-reaching reform.

The Community Reinvestment Act, passed during the Clinton administration, had forced the banking industry to write "sub-prime" mortgages for people whose credit ratings and financial resources indicated they were bad risks. "Under Clinton's HUD secretary, Andrew Cuomo... (B)anks were effectively rewarded for throwing out sound underwriting standards and writing loans to those who were at high risk of defaulting," write economists Stephen Moore and Lawrence Kudlow. "…These new HUD rules lowered down payments from the traditional 20 percent to 3 percent by 1995 and zero down-payments by 2000. In the Clinton push to issue home loans to lower income borrowers, Fannie Mae and Freddie Mac made it common practice to virtually end credit documentation; low credit scores were disregarded, and income and job history were thrown aside."

And of course, almost all these borrowers went under water when the housing house of cards came crashing down.

Needless to say, no one had pushed the Clinton Administration with greater fervor to enact the financially suicidal policies than activists like Obama, some of whom actually characterized sub-prime loans aimed at increasing black home ownership as reparations for slavery and segregation. Never mind that it would be by government largesse, without the real work of building generational wealth other ethnic groups had done, and otherwise following the tried-and-true path of building nuclear families and family businesses through education, work and savings.

Recently out of Harvard Law school and not yet in electoral politics, Obama was working in the Clinton years as a "civil rights" lawyer in the Chicago firm Milner, Barnhill & Galland, and was part of the problem. Indeed, he was a member of the team representing 186 black Chicagoans in a class action mortgage discrimination lawsuit against Citibank. In the settlement of *Buycks-Roberson v. Citibank*

Fed. Sav. Bank, his clients got their mortgages, with Citibank paying the winning side's fees. But his clients got the win without learning the far more valuable lesson of wealth building via behaviors and habits which lead to good credit ratings and the building of healthy nest eggs.

The end result? According to a *Daily Caller* article, by 2012 only 19 of Obama's 186 clients still had their homes. About half the others had gone bankrupt or had their homes in foreclosure.

Unsurprisingly, by then more than a few of these were wishing they'd taken a different course. "If you see some people don't make enough money to afford the mortgage," said one, of the banks that had been forced to act against their better judgement, "why should you give them a loan? There should be some type of regulation against giving people loans they can't afford."

Though Obama apologists would later minimize his role in the damning case, documents showed that his bill came to $23,000, representing 138 hours of work.

Still, Obama was the opposite of dismayed by the 2008 crash that he and his crowd had a large hand in making. Not only was it a huge factor in his victory over John McCain, but in grievously wounding the free-market system he despised, it gave him great range of action to introduce the sorts of "reforms" that would otherwise have been unimaginable.

Within Obama's first year:

— The Democrats in control of the U.S. Senate had increased the federal debt limit to $13 trillion, leading to runaway federal spending that had the national debt at $11.95 trillion.

— The Federal Reserve was changing rules on compensation for executives at the 28 largest banks in the country so as to discourage "excessive risk-taking" – a policy that ultimately resulted in almost no one getting a "speculative" bank loan, and seriously undermining hopes for small business startups. Every year Obama was in office, there were fewer businesses operating in America than the previous year.

While the understandable first reaction of many was that the executives suffering those steep pay cuts were only getting their just desserts, hardly every such executive was guilty of malfeasance, and the virtuous were punished with the culpable.

— The federal "pay czar," Kenneth Feinberg imposed draconian cuts in executive compensation at such firms as Bank of America Corp., American International Group Inc., Citigroup Inc., General Motors, GMAC, Chrysler and Chrysler Financial. The cuts involved were said to wipe out as much as 90 percent of salaries and as much as 50 percent of total compensation.

But, then, Obamunism isn't just about collective salvation. It dictates collective punishment, too.

Many of America's larger banks had fallen under the government thumb in the first place only after being pressured to accept federal TARP money they didn't want or need. "I wouldn't like to use the word 'threat,' Minnesota-based TCF Financial chairman and CEO Bill Cooper said of administration tactics, "but what they said was that they were going to give this money only to the strong banks. And if you didn't take the money, you'd be recognized as a weak bank."

According to Cooper – who took the money but returned it early – in places like Minnesota, federal action made things worse, predicting "we'll pay the piper down years from now."

By December of 2009, Obama was dragging prominent bankers to the White House and berating them for the tightening of credit markets and the economic asthma attack that was causing.

His contempt was palpable. "I did not run for office to be helping out a bunch of fat cat bankers on Wall Street," he'd told *60 Minutes* a few days earlier, and in the White House he proceeded to lecture the bankers on their obligations now that the government had shoveled all that money at them. "(G)iven the difficulty business people are having as lending has declined," he intoned, "and given the exceptional assistance banks received to get them through a difficult time, we expect them to explore every responsible way to help get our economy moving again."

But Obama's cajoling and bullying couldn't alter the sorts of economic realities with which the bankers at the White House meeting were all too familiar. "He can say what he wants, but we're not going to go back to the kind of lending that put us in this mess," said one.

Their caution was obviously justified. Both commercial and residential real estate were depressed, and the stock market was down by 30 percent from its high two years prior.

And as Obama's minions in the Senate continued to open the door to ever-higher levels of federal debt, the debt burden per American household already sat at close to $100,000 with projections that the number would nearly double over the next decade.

And, indeed, by the time Obama left the White House seven years later, the per-household debt burden had ballooned to $166,000.

By then, Obama had blown $787 billion on an unmitigated disaster of a stimulus package. This failure would later be carbon-copied in Joe Biden's Obama Redux presidency in the fraudulently named American Rescue Plan.

Then there were the massive number of tax dollars he set on fire on wasteful giveaways like that to the solar panel maker, Solyndra. Why? Because, as he proclaimed in 2010, "The true engine of economic growth will always be companies like Solyndra."

It's doubtful that even Obama himself believed that. Ron Klain, later to be Joe Biden's first chief of staff, was a key advisor to Obama while serving as Biden's vice-presidential chief of staff, and he was in on the debate over how tightly Obama should embrace Solyndra. In an e-mail from Klain to Valerie Jarrett subsequently produced by *USA Today*, it was clear the Obama Team was fully aware the green agenda made zero financial sense – and that it and other such companies "will be belly-up by election day 2012."

They didn't care whether it was good business. Their definition of good business is wholly different than yours.

Their business was to push leftist ideology in the marketplace. Before he was done, more than fifty clean-energy companies Obama backed as part of the disastrous ARRA stimulus plan in 2009 would end up bankrupt or otherwise in deep financial trouble. Solyndra itself went belly up less than a year after receiving a $535 million Department of Energy loan, laying off 1,100 workers.

Yet undeterred – or, more likely, encouraged – Obama proceeded to ram through that federal seizure of the medical sector that 54 percent of the American people rejected in polling.

He pushed for a cap-and-trade bill involving, among other things, a $3.6 trillion tax increase on gasoline, and though it didn't pass, the thinking behind it stayed on.

Obama and his Democrat lickspittles in Congress certainly weren't imposing principles of austerity on themselves or others within the federal apparatus; those principles were only good for the private firms they were in the process of nationalizing.

Again, this wasn't just incompetence, it was driven by an all-consuming belief in "clean energy," and the readiness, even eagerness, to enforce it by outright tyranny. Their view was government had the not just the power, but the absolute right to dictate to private citizens how they run their businesses, from how much they and their workers were to be paid, to the ways they were permitted to contract with other parties. That property rights and the freedom to engage in economic activity have always been bedrock principles of

American life going back to the Declaration of Independence was, for them, a mere bump in the road to be overcome.

Obama's unapologetic hostility toward foundational aspects of capitalism was in some ways a reprise of FDR's class warfare of the Depression years. Back then, as today, the left was convinced, notes Amity Shlaes in *The Forgotten Man*, her brilliant account of that era, that the economy "could not revive without extensive intervention by Washington." However, in FDR's time, businesses could sit on their cash and invest long term, waiting out the radicals, as FDR's sluggish economy stagnated.

Obama was not just willing, but far more able, to bend them to his will.

Among the many instances of untrammeled federal abuses of power under Obama, one that drew particular notice occurred on August 24, 2011, when federal agents with rifles and tactical gear raided Gibson Guitar Corp.'s facilities in Nashville and Memphis, Tennessee. The feds shut down the factory floor, sent the employees home, and hauled off all the wood on the premises.

Why? According to Eric Holder's Justice Department, Gibson was illegally importing wood from India, in violation of the Lacey Act, passed more than a century before to stop illegal trade in flowers and fauna. Not illegally according to American law – illegally according to *Indian* and *Madagascan* law.

Except it soon came out that those governments had approved the export of the East Indian rosewood Gibson was using. Gibson asserted that not only had they fully complied with all the foreign laws, but they were compliant with an industry standard for "responsible management of the world's forests."

It soon also emerged that Gibson's principal competitors, Fender and C.F. Martin, were also using rosewood in their guitars, yet they hadn't been raided or had their material and products seized.

What was going on?

Answer: Gibson's CEO, Henry Juszkiewicz, was a Republican donor, an anomaly in the industry, while his counterparts at the other companies, were Democratic donors, with Martin's Chris Martin IV having given more than $35,000 to Democratic candidates and the Democratic National Committee.

Nonetheless, to reclaim their property and avoid the expense of an interminable legal fight, Gibson ended up settling the case with the government for around $300,000 - $262,000 of which was a write down of the government seizure of the wood, which ultimately was returned to the company, and another $50,000 in a "community service payment" to the National Fish and Wildlife Foundation — for forest conservation.

In a glorious show of defiance, with the returned wood, Gibson crafted the Government Series II Les Paul special edition guitar.

Nonetheless, in such an environment, few in the business world were prepared to defy the Obama administration and go through comparable hell.

In fact, the cudgel Obama held over business – and was all too ready to use – led to the first stirrings of the horror that would come to be called Woke Capitalism. Future presidential candidate Vivek Ramaswamy notes in his book *Woke, Inc.*, the extraordinary favoritism Obama and his goons lavished on those overtly sympathetic to the cause – and the punishment doled out to those, like Gibson, who resisted the government's power. He cites, for example, the massive settlement, nearly $17 billion, that Obama's attorney general Eric Holder announced in 2014 after a Justice Department lawsuit against Bank of America for its part in causing the financial crisis.

About $6 billion of that money went to the U.S. government in reimbursement for bailing out the banks. But the other $11 billion that was supposed to go toward "consumer relief?" Not only did much of it go instead to Democratic-favored nonprofits, but it actually ended up being far less than $11 billion, because the DOJ offered banks a huge discount whenever they played ball and "donated" that money to those nonprofits. Most of the settlements gave banks double or triple credit toward their fine for every dollar they donated to these nonprofits—for instance, a Bank of America $1.15 million "donation" to the National Urban League counted as $2.6 million toward meeting its settlement obligation, and every $1.5 million to La Raza counted as $3.5 million of consumer relief.

In short, "the Obama DOJ slammed big banks with massive fines so it could trumpet that it was sending tons of relief to consumers. Then it told banks they could pay less than half that much if they donated the money to Obama's favorite nonprofits instead."

Once companies like Bank of America had been yoked to the woke agenda, it was almost a fire-and-forget situation. It wouldn't be long before BOA was discriminating against gun-sellers and de-banking them, so zealous were they as repurposed corporate terminators.

Then there was the sue-and-settle tactic favored by Eric Holder's Justice Department and, among other federal agencies, the EPA, long a repository for otherwise-unemployable anti-capitalist loons eager to sap the private sector in which they are manifestly unqualified to serve. The Obama administration turbocharged the EPA and set it loose on a bacchanalian lawfare spree through the economy. Between 2009 and 2012 alone, the EPA entered into more than sixty settlements at a cost to the economy of tens of billions of dollars.

It was essentially a sting operation, with honest corporate citizens as the mark. The way it worked was that EPA-favored left-wing nonprofits like the Sierra Club or the Environmental Defense Fund would sue the federal government alleging all kinds of dubious harms – and rather than defend itself, the government would roll over, agreeing to pay out massive settlements in our tax dollars to Obama's ideological pals. Too, they'd agree to institute policies that could never have been passed by Congress – especially not after the Republicans took over the House majority in the 2010 Tea Party wave election.

So potentially damaging was such a hit on a company that much of corporate America rolled over for Obama and his allies, or went paying – financially or with their souls – for protection.

That's how we ended up with a Gillette ad featuring a father teaching a little "trans" boy how to shave. A huge number of the legacy American corporations, the blue-chip stocks whose founders have been dead and gone for a century or more are now run by functionaries readily cowed into believing their brands can stay relevant and profitable and not turn into JC Penney or Braniff Airlines by means of caving to the left.

It's like Lenin said: the capitalist will sell you the rope by which you hang him. Except Lenin was a bloodthirsty dunce compared to Obama, who understood it's better to turn the capitalist into your own personal, well-heeled zombie rather than shoot him and drop him in a ditch. You can always do that later.

A handful of privately-held companies still run by the entrepreneurs who built them were tougher to co-opt. David Green, the founder and CEO of Hobby Lobby, the Oklahoma-based national chain of craft stores, is an evangelical Christian and a staunch pro-lifer, so when Obamacare mandated that all companies of size include the "morning-after pill" in their health insurance coverage, he sued the federal government – and, after a years-long battle which ended at the Supreme Court, he won.

But overwhelmingly, corporate America went along with all the Obamacare mandates which jammed leftist cultural aggressions into federal policy.

Wall Street caved with particular fervor, shaken to its foundations by the two-month-long Occupy protest in the neighborhood that spawned imitations in more than 100 cities, spreading the not-entirely-crazy message that American politics and economics only benefited the top one percent. True to form, Obama took full advantage. "I think it expresses the frustrations that the American people feel," he solemnly told an October 2011 press conference promoting his American Jobs Act. "We had the biggest financial crisis since the Great Depression – huge collateral damage through-out the country, all across main street. And yet, you are still seeing some of the same folks who acted irresponsibly trying to fight efforts to crack down on abusive practices that got us in the situation in the first place."

A month later he delivered the Occupy crowd their greatest "win" by canceling the Keystone XL pipeline, though almost no one noted that the real winner was Obama's own chief supporter in the financial sector, mega-donor Warren Buffet, whose Burlington Northern Santa Fe Railroad would now transport south the oil from Canadian tar sands that otherwise would have flowed through the pipeline.

It is not for nothing that Wall Street money which in the past had gone to Republicans by ratios as high as four-to-one, now began conspicuously flowing in the other direction; so much so that in 2020, Biden's take would total fully 70% of the $2.9 billion lavished by the financial sector in political contributions.

By the end of Obama's second term, the American economy was basically in the same shape as those hollowed and bailed-out firms now ruled by government diktat: dead broke, beaten down, drained of talent, direction and ambition, in permanent decline compared to their hungrier and more aggressive competitors (many of whom resided in China). Team Obama had brought corporate America to heel, tamed it and turned it into a domesticated beast of burden for the Hard Left agenda.

To a certain extent that would reverse itself during at least the first three years of Donald Trump's presidency. But once the Obamites were back in the Biden administration things got worse than ever. And the relationship between the left and corporate America has now metastasized into what Ramaswamy rightly calls the greatest threat to American freedom ever brought to bear.

We're in a situation today where it's harder than ever to finance, staff and operate a small business. And more money sits in fewer hands in America than even during the age of the robber barons of the late 19th century.

And how did Obamanomics work out for the black community?

According to the Federal Reserve, from 2010 to 2013, median net worth — a household's assets minus its liabilities — for white households increased 2.4%. Black net worth? It fell from $16,600 to $11,000, a four-year drop of 34 percent.

Indeed, Obama's economy proved a major factor in further souring race relations – for the pain inflicted was not just economic but psychological. As the profligate giveaways of the Sixties War on Poverty left in their wake mass disillusion and bitterness, with black neighborhoods nationwide going up in flames in its aftermath, so Obama's redistributive, corrective governmental administration and its enervating effect on the economy inevitably led to greater class envy, and increased demands for more and better government handouts. Indeed, Obamacare and free cell phones produced greatly increased calls for the ultimate prize, reparations.

But, of course, even those would never be enough. Because just giving people largesse without building a healthy environment for achievement and upward mobility is a recipe only for more envy, hopelessness and rage.

Yet all this, too was intentional. For it turns out that a stagnant economy increasingly dependent on government makes for not only a more malleable electorate, but a more malleable business community also.

It is no coincidence that Big Business is today as crucial a piece of the Democrats' coalition as Big Poverty.

CHAPTER 13

RACIAL PYROMANIA

Give Obama credit for this: he was a multi-tasker. Even as he was shaking America to its political and economic foundations, he was taking a jackhammer to a widely shared consensus arrived at through a half-century of pain, struggle and introspection on the most intractable issue of all – race.

Obviously, profound disagreements remained over contentious issues like affirmative action. And, yes, anger-fueled animosity still simmered in the hard hearts of more than a few. Yet those were increasingly on the fringes, for the progress in racial reconciliation achieved in America since the bloody mayhem of the civil rights movement had been nothing short of remarkable. Indeed, the condition of race relations was unprecedented. By the turn of the twenty-first century, even the sharpest disagreements were invariably about means, not ends. Ronald Reagan had designated Martin Luther King's birthday a federal holiday back in 1983, and his dream was the aspiration of the entire nation – and moving by degrees toward fulfillment.

"I have a dream," King had proclaimed in his legendary 1963 address, "that one day even the state of Mississippi, a state sweltering with the heat of injustice, sweltering with the heat of oppression will be transformed into an oasis of freedom and justice.

"I have a dream that my four little children will one day live in a nation where they will not be judged by the color of their skin but by the content of their character."

Astonishingly – file under Only in America – Charles Evers, the brother of another civil rights martyr, Medgar, and himself the first black mayor of a Mississippi town since Reconstruction, could sit in his Jackson office in 2007 and, pointing to a photo on the wall, tell an interviewer: "Once I couldn't walk down the street with a white woman. See that, now I got a white son-in-law and white grandkids."

Barack Obama knew he had to campaign as representing the next – in fact, as the final and decisive – step in this saga of racial healing. As the advertised son of an African immigrant rather than someone with a personal history rooted in slavery and Jim Crow, he was at pains to link himself to the civil rights struggle. Gearing up for the race, he made a well-publicized trip to Selma, Alabama, walking solemnly across the infamous Edmund Pettus Bridge, site of the vicious 1963 police beating of unarmed protestors, then addressing a local black congregation. He spoke of how under the British, Barack Obama, Sr., too, had suffered the ravages of discrimination. "So don't tell me I don't have a claim on Selma, Alabama," he proclaimed. "Don't tell me I'm not coming home to Selma, Alabama."

Obama ran, and won, on that basis. Conservative essayist Shelby Steele, himself of mixed race, neatly summed it up: "Americans bargained with Obama: if Obama put race in the past, Americans were willing to put him in the White House."

But in that crucial sense, as in so many others, it was a campaign of deceit and obfuscation, and it wasn't long before at least some voters grasped they'd been duped.

On Election Day 2008, a handful of toughs from the New Black Panther Party (NBPP) showed up outside a racially-mixed-but-mostly-black polling precinct with truncheons. Hurling epithets like "white devil," they intimidated white voters into not going inside.

One woman of unsuitable melanin content reported being sneered at: "You're about to be ruled by the black man, cracker!"

Although it was one of the clearest cases of voter intimidation in America in decades, and it had been captured on video, it was a single episode in the grand tapestry of the national election, and it might have been dismissed as not terribly meaningful, and easily handled. With George W. Bush's administration still in place, the Department of Justice

(DOJ) dutifully moved to sue two NBPP members, Minister King Samir Shabazz and Jerry Jackson, for voter intimidation.

That should have been that. But immediately on taking office, Obama's attorney general, Eric Holder dismissed the suit against Jackson and greatly narrowed the one against Shabazz. And before long, the cases disintegrated entirely.

America was under new management. Black radicals would now be treated with kid gloves.

The dismissal prompted a pair of DOJ lawyers, Christopher Coates and J. Christian Adams, to resign in disgust. Adams, who has gone on to become one of the nation's preeminent authorities on voter irregularity, charged that the New Black Panther Party case was dropped because it was now policy in the DOJ that black violators of election laws were to be treated differently.

At the time, such a notion seemed preposterous; America was a nation of laws. Whatever happened with this case, it had to be anomalous.

Today, in a time when underclass criminality goes unpunished in every progressive-run city in America, everyone who is paying attention knows better.

Obama made abundantly clear that he intended to take a very different line on race his first summer in office, when he turned what should have been discounted as an unfortunate misunderstanding into an excuse for a presidential scolding of whites for their deep-seated racism.

On July 16, 2009, black Harvard professor Henry Louis "Skip" Gates, Jr. – director of the school's Hutchins Center for African and African American Research and soon to become better known as the host of such PBS programs as "Finding Your Roots" – was spotted by a white Cambridge police sergeant named James Crowley trying to break into a house that turned out to be his own. At that point, accounts of what occurred sharply diverged. Crowley claimed that when he approached to investigate, the professor first refused to provide proof he lived in the house, then quickly became abusive, shouting, "Why, because I'm a black man in America?" and continuing to be uncooperative. Gates claimed it was the sergeant who was abusive, repeatedly refusing to give his name or badge number. What neither disputed is that the kerfuffle quicky escalated, with Crowley arresting Gates for disorderly conduct.

In short order, the episode became a national story, with the eminent Harvard professor maintaining he'd been racially profiled by the blue-collar white cop, with progressives (including the Black Congressional Caucus) supporting Gates and police unions around the country lining up behind Crowley. The Cambridge Police Commissioner Robert C. Haas defended his officer as having fully followed protocol, and it helped Gates case not at all when it turned out that, far from a northern version of a swaggering 60's small town Southern sheriff, Crowley taught a class on racial profiling at the Lowell Police Academy. "I have nothing but the highest respect for him as a police officer," Academy Director Thomas Fleming, who is black, told the Associated

Press. "He is very professional, and he is a good role model for the young recruits in the police academy,"

Obama weighed in several days later, at a press conference –siding with Gates, and describing the case as emblematic of the deep racial divide in America. "I think it's fair to say, number one, any of us would be pretty angry," he said. "Number two, that the Cambridge police acted stupidly in arresting somebody when there was already proof that they were in their own home. And number three, what I think we know separate and apart from this incident is that there is a long history in this country of African Americans and Latinos being stopped by law enforcement disproportionately. That's just a fact."

Never had he so badly let slip the mask of studied moderation.

While attacking cops has long been *pro forma* among black nationalists and 60s radicals, never had it been done from the bully pulpit of the White House, and Obama's performance at the news conferences generated more than a little shocked surprise.

Recognizing the magnitude of his error, he quickly did an about-face, seeking to reemerge as a Healer-in-Chief. He announced what would come to be known as the "beer summit," and had the antagonists to the White House, where in view of the press, they sat at a table over brews and peanuts and appeared to make nice. "When he's not arresting you," Gates afterward joked to *The New York Times*, "Sergeant Crowley is a really likable guy."

But as the real Barack Obama had made a brief, unaccustomed appearance, at least some damage had been done. According to Pew Research, in the aftermath of the episode, white support for Obama, which had stood at 53 percent, declined by seven points, and in coming years, it would fall sharply further.

In no small part, that would be due to his administration's increasingly open hostility toward cops. Nor was it just the police he viewed with such obvious suspicion; it was the very meaning of the "law and order" he, like they, had sworn to uphold.

As a radical, the new president had an entirely different view of a fair and just society than did the law enforcement personnel and the majority of the judges who enforced the laws on the books and – for that matter, of the vast majority of ordinary citizens of all races. He had been raised to believe, and later preached as a community organizer, that the entire system was stacked against people of color; and that for all the high-minded talk of "equal justice under the law," racial minorities would never get their just due unless and until progressive government recognized the fact, and its causes, and moved to meaningfully rectify the centuries of abuse at the heart of the American story. Unless and until that happened, the struggle of the oppressed against the system was right, even when it involved what the less ideologically evolved regarded as criminality.

Indeed, today, thanks to the Soros prosecutors in Democrat cities, we see Obama's answer to rising crime, especially when carried out by young black men – played out in daily practice – not severe penalties, or even penalties at all, but trying to be sympathetic and tolerant of the rage that's caused them to act out.

If anyone doubted this was Obama's view, the 2012 Trayvon Martin case should have eliminated all doubt.

When it was first reported that the black Sanford, Florida, teenager had been shot and killed by a neighbor-hood watch volunteer named George Zimmerman, the story seemed pretty straightforward. After all, Martin was a juvenile delinquent who had been suspended from a Miami high school three times for criminal behavior, including an assault on a bus driver, and for possession of a bag of women's jewelry and a "burglary tool" he claimed wasn't his. It was exactly the sort of behavior neighborhood watch types had been taught to spot.

Staying with his mother while serving his third school suspension, that rainy late February night, Martin went to a nearby convenience store. But, as he made his way home through a middle-class gated neighborhood that had lately seen a surge in crime, Zimmerman spotted Martin rushing from covered carport to eaves to porches in a way that suggested he was casing houses. A wannabe cop and sometime private security guard of mixed, half-Colombian ancestry, Zimmerman followed him for a time in his SUV and then called him in to the police.

From the transcript of the call:

Zimmerman: *Hey we've had some break-ins in my neighborhood, and there's a real suspicious guy, uh, [near] Retreat View Circle, um, the best address I can give you is 111 Retreat View Circle. This guy looks like he's up to no good, or he's on drugs or something. It's raining and he's just walking around, looking about."*

Zimmerman got out of his truck and confronted Martin, and that confrontation went badly. Martin, who was six feet tall and a muscular 180 pounds, knocked Zimmerman down and proceeded to beat him in an MMA ground-and-pound style.

As Martin was beating the daylights out of him, Zimmerman found the gun in his waistband and shot his assailant in the chest. Martin died shortly thereafter.

The toxicology report following Martin's death showed he was high at the time. He also had bloody knuckles, proving he'd been punching Zimmerman. Later poring through Martin's social media paper trail, conservative media outlets found evidence he was a frequent drug user and probably a low-level dealer. Video of the night in question, particularly surveillance video from outside of the 7-11 where he'd bought Skittles and a can of Arizona Watermelon (ingredients, together with cough syrup, in a homemade intoxicating concoction called sizzurp or lean or Purple Drank which Martin's social media revealed he was a frequent user of), showed his physical movements as wobbly or swaying, consistent with inebriation.

For a couple of weeks after Trayvon Martin's death, the case, a clear-cut matter of self-defense, received little national attention. Local prosecutors saw nothing to charge Zimmerman with.

But then activists got a hold of it, and in short order the Obama-Holder Justice Department dispatched a unit with a history of anti-white racial advocacy to help facilitate protestors calling for Zimmerman's prosecution. A major rally was headlined by activist Al Sharpton, who threatened to call for civil disobedience if Zimmerman was not arrested.

And it was on.

The Martin family's attorney was one Benjamin Crump, who played a large part in ginning up the media circus. Both Trayvon's parents quit their jobs to become full time "activists," and Crump and his partner Daryl Parks organized marches at which they were prominently featured. To anyone who would listen, which was pretty much every reporter on the scene, Crump accused the local cops of a cover-up, and repeatedly insisted that race was the motive behind the shooting of Martin, something Zimmerman passionately denied.

Among the media, leftist black reporters stood out for their stridency. Ta-Nehisi Coates at the *Atlantic*, Charles M. Blow at the *New York Times*, and Trymaine Lee at the *Huffington Post* all wrote in passionate terms about the racist atrocity happening in Sanford, and before long their white brethren were following them.

In news reports, Martin was almost always shown in an old photo as an angelic-looking 12-year-old, rather than as the powerful fully-grown young man with a mouth full of metallic teeth he'd become. Zimmerman was first widely described as a white supremacist – and when his ethnic origin became clear, as a "white Hispanic." Either way, the night of the shooting he'd supposedly been out for blood.

Enter Obama, to pour kerosene on the fire. "If I had a son," he announced soberly, "he'd look like Trayvon."

And when Zimmerman was acquitted the following year, Obama doubled down. "Trayvon Martin could have been me 35 years ago."

This was an absurdity. Obama was a middle-class kid in Hawaii, attending a fancy private school, with no hint of a criminal past beyond smoking grass. Martin was a budding outlaw with multiple charges on his way out of a public high school who got himself in a fight to the death with someone holding a gun.

Worse than stupid, Obama's evoking of his past self in this context was tragic. A graduate of the nation's leading schools, who'd ascended to the very top, no one better exemplified America as a land of opportunity. If ever there was an individual positioned to be a role model for black underclass kids, he should have been it.

But he couldn't be that kind of figure because it's not what he believes, and never has been. It's just that this fundamental truth had been concealed by an adoring press.

Indeed, back in 2007, when he showed up in Selma to shore up his racial *bona fides*, not one journalist reported that as Obama strode across the Edmund Pettus Bridge, he was flanked by a pair of Black Panthers, fists in the air.

CHAPTER 14

ANTI-COP, PRO-CRIMINAL

T oday, the idea that cops pose a deadly threat to black people is so pervasive that even reasonably informed people believe that hundreds, even thousands, of innocent blacks die every year at the hands of trigger-happy police.

It is a despicable lie. But like so many lies at the heart of the left/Democratic belief system, it is a lie with a political purpose.

The truth is that there is zero statistical evidence, *none,* to support the claim that blacks are targeted by law enforcement with deadly force more than individuals of other races.

Indeed, if anything, thanks to Obama's time in the White House, the opposite is true, as cops well know that in encounters with black people, their careers or even freedom are potentially on the line. So they have become far more tentative even in the face of black criminality than they once were – and ought to be. Particularly in progressive cites, where cops are especially vulnerable, the result is that life is now a lot more dangerous for law-abiding citizens of all races.

No one has written more extensively on the question of policing and race than The Manhattan Institute's Heather MacDonald, and no one more compellingly makes the case that virtually everything most people are sure they know about racist cops is errant nonsense.

And dangerous, society-killing nonsense at that.

MacDonald points to a 2019 study in the *Proceedings of the National Academy of Sciences,* for instance, that closely examined every officer-involved fatal shootings in the year 2015 – there were 917, involving more than 650 police departments. Though the study's authors were left-of-center academics, professors at Michigan State University and the University of Maryland at College Park, what they found conclusively contradicted the anti-cop narrative. It determined that white police officers are in fact no more likely than black or Hispanic officers to shoot black civilians, and that across America, white cops kill *unarmed* blacks no more than a handful of times a year.

It further clarified that it is violent crime that leads to almost all police shootings, not the race of either officer or the criminal. The more often cops encounter violent suspects from a racial group, the greater the chance that members of that racial group will be shot by a police officer; but that is an entirely different thing than the killing of innocent, or unarmed, individuals of color. A 2015 study indicated that between 90 and 95 percent of those of any race shot by officers were shot in the act of attacking police or other citizens, and fully 90 percent of those were armed with a weapon.

"In 2015," writes MacDonald, of the media's highly selective reporting on the issue, "the white victims of fatal police shootings included a 50-year-old suspect in a domestic assault in Tuscaloosa, Ala., who ran at the officer with a spoon; a 28-year-old driver in Des Moines, Iowa, who exited his car and walked quickly toward an officer after a car chase; and a 21-year-old suspect in a grocery-store robbery in Akron, Ohio, who had escaped on a bike and who did not remove his hand from his waistband when ordered to do so. Had any of these victims been black, the media and activists would probably have jumped on their stories and added their names to the roster of victims of police racism. Instead, because they are white, they are unknown..."

It is only because the media pay such extraordinary attention to every racially charged incident, (however complicated the circumstances or uncertain the underlying facts), in contrast to how relatively little they give others, that ordinary people believe there are so many unarmed blacks killed by white cops.

In fact, once crime rates are taken into account, the statistics show that if there's any bias, it is against *white* civilians. Fifty-five percent of the victims in the study were white, 27 percent were black, and 19 percent were Hispanic.

Nor are the numbers in the 2015 study unusual. The same dynamic holds for the entire 21st century to date. The facts on this are so clear-cut that in July 2020 even the *Washington Post*, one of the most liberal newspapers in America, acknowledged this point in an article detailing the statistics.

This is not to say there are not higher overall rates of black criminality. Whites are assaulted and murdered by blacks at a far higher rate than the reverse; and the overwhelming majority of violent acts against blacks – 93% – are committed by other blacks.

Meanwhile, what is beyond question is that the Obama years made life more hazardous for police officers of all races. Justice Department statistics show ambushes of cops climbed 25 percent between 2008 to 2013 over rates of the previous ten years, and in 2016, Obama's last year in office, the number killed in the line of duty mushroomed 56 percent over 2015. A full third of those were attacks in which cops were ambushed.

These facts are almost never reported by the same legacy media sure to be all over any fatality involving the police shooting of a black person, especially if video is involved. For each such instance is a potential opportunity to cue up the narrative of racism run amok.

During the Obama years, more than a few such cases, nourished by a lazy and credulous leftist media, exploded into national stories.

There was the 2014 case of Eric Garner, a mostly-unemployed, morbidly obese 41-year old semiprofessional criminal who died outside a Staten Island convenience store after a police officer put him in a chokehold, the cops having been called by the store's manager complaining Garner was selling "loosey" cigarettes outside the premises. To be sure, his "crime" was penny ante. But he had been resisting arrest as the cops struggled to get him into the police car, and according to the coroner's report, his poor physical condition also played a significant part in the outcome.

But there was video, and the story dominated the New York media for over a year. Although charges against the officer were eventually dropped, he was fired by the NYPD.

Garner's family, meanwhile, sued the city of New York and collected $5.9 million.

Then there was the 2016 case of 37-year-old Alton Sterling, a career criminal with a 20-year record, who'd been in and out of prison for offenses ranging from petty theft to child molestation. Sterling was standing outside a convenience store in Baton Rouge, Louisiana, ostensibly selling bootleg CD's, a classic front for drug dealing. In violation of his parole, he had a gun, which he brandished at a recalcitrant customer, and the cops were called. While grappling with the cops, Sterling reached for his pistol, and he was shot dead.

Media reports of the murder of the "innocent" CD salesman soon launched mass protests. A few weeks later, an activist with the Nation of Islam and New Black Panthers came to Baton Rouge from Texas and shot six law enforcement officers in an ambush. Three were killed immediately;

another, Officer Nick Tullier of the Baton Rouge Police Department, succumbed to his wounds several years later.

The Sterling case also set off a second black radical on an anti-cop spree, Micah Xavier Johnson, who shot five police officers in Dallas.

For their part, the officers involved in the Alton Sterling case were found not guilty by both federal and state officials. Nonetheless, once again, the officer who fired the shot lost his job, and once again, the dead man's family cashed in, this time to the tune of $4.5 million from the city. Baton Rouge also had to pay another million-plus to the protesters arrested in the violent demonstrations that followed the shooting.

Hardly incidentally, as MacDonald points out, "the anti-cop narrative deflects attention away from solving the real criminal-justice problem, which is high rates of *black-on-black* victimization. Blacks die of homicide at eight times the rate of non-Hispanic whites, overwhelmingly killed not by cops, not by whites, but by other blacks. The Democratic candidates should get their facts straight and address that issue. Until they do, their talk of racial justice will ring hollow."

Except they don't care that it rings hollow. It works for them among the audiences they reach with it – urban blacks and guilt-ridden white leftists, typically single women with college degrees granted in subjects of questionable market value.

And in Barack Obama, they had a president whom they could love and trust without reservation, as readily overlooking his twenty years in Jeremiah Wright's church as they were eager to embrace his narrative of cops as agents of oppression within the black community.

Obama spent his entire presidency lighting fires around urban policing, subtly and not so subtly pushing anti-*white* racism, and of course never taking responsibility for the calamitous results. But it would inevitably lead to the movement to defund cops, and the massive spikes in violent crime to follow.

The naïve might wonder why the Democrats stick to such an obviously destructive narrative on race, one that stresses victimhood while keeping the focus off (and aggravating) the real problems plaguing black inner cities: spiraling crime rates, fatherless homes, schools that don't teach, hopelessness in every guise.

The answer is simple as it is cynical: power.

As the successor party to the old CPUSA/Democratic Socialists, today's Democrats understand that runaway crime in the beleaguered communities they run increases their control. It gives them an entree to endlessly flog so-called systemic racism – even as rising crime runs off the middle-class voters who might otherwise vote out machine Democrat urban socialists. When the local private economy is obliterated by the criminals, what's left is (1) government, and (2) municipal unions and community organizing types lobbying it for ever more *largesse*, when they're not shaking down what remains of the business community.

From such a perspective, it's not hard to grasp why progressives tend to be so curiously friendly to criminals, and indifferent to their victims. They share a contempt for the values of thrift and hard work that characterize more decent and productive people.

And Obama – he of "You didn't build that" – was their natural champion. A racialist of the first order, unremittingly hostile to the society he'd elected to lead, he had all his life been aligned with those most interested in tearing it down.

Before he was done, his Justice Department, in concert with progressive Democratic mayors, would embark on a program of defenestrating urban police departments across the country. The chosen means were consent decrees – agreements fashioned by sympathetic judges to curb the power and reach of local law enforcement.

The cities involved were generally in economic and demographic decline, with cultural breakdown resulting in commensurate increases in crime; which is to say, their police departments were already overwhelmed and beleaguered. When they were further kneecapped by the courts, inevitably, bad things happened.

Take the Tamir Rice tragedy in Cleveland.

A 12-year-old kid, Rice was in a park in a dangerous area of the city, playing with a toy gun, when he was confronted by a pair of Cleveland cops. Someone had called 911, reporting there was a man — "probably a juvenile" — pointing a gun — "probably fake" — at people on the playground. Tragically, however, the dispatcher failed to relay to the responding officers the likelihood that it was a child with a toy, and when they spotted Rice with what looked like a real gun, they thought they might have a mass shooting on their hands. One of them shot the boy and killed him.

A local grand jury, citing evidence the officers "repeatedly and consistently… gave Tamir multiple commands to show his hands before shooting, and both officers repeatedly and consistently said that they saw Tamir reaching for his gun," refused to issue indictments against either, (though of course one was later fired anyway.)

But by then, in fact, even before the conclusion of the investigation into Tamir's death, Holder's DOJ had swooped in and, using the tragedy as an excuse, pressured the city of Cleveland into a consent decree. "There is reasonable cause to believe that the Cleveland Division of Police engages in a pattern and practice of using excessive force," claimed Obama's wingman, and the DOJ followed with a report savaging the Cleveland force for "poor and dangerous tactics," pistol-whippings, guns fired at "unarmed or fleeing suspects," and supervisors "all the way up the chain of command" who "approved the use of force as appropriate."

The consent decree enforced upon the CPD greatly restricted the actions of its officers, who began quitting in droves. What had once been a strong urban police force was gutted. But the consent decree remained, and as late as 2022, a local TV station would report that "(s)even years after monitoring started, the 144-page semi-annual report says Cleveland Police are still struggling…Thanks to the low salary and morale, the department is losing more officers than it's hiring…"

"The quickest we can get out of this decree, the better it will be for the police department and the taxpayers so we can use that money to reinvest back in, long-term,' (Mayor) Bibb said last month. But the decision is not up to him. It's over when a federal judge decides it's done."

In short, thanks to Obama's DOJ, Cleveland is caught in a vicious circle of ineffectual policing and rising crime that leads to more ineffectual policing.

So are at least 20 other Democrat-run municipalities, whose police departments were gutted by similar Obama-era anti-cop decrees, that left morale plummeting and working conditions so awful that cops have fled en masse to Republican-run suburbs, or red states like Florida, where they have support from the public and the political class.

Undoubtably, the most notorious race case on Obama's watch was the one touched off on August 9, 2014, in the St. Louis suburb of Ferguson, Missouri, by the police killing of Michael Brown.

An 18-year-old recent high school graduate and would-be rap musician, Brown stood a mountainous 6'4" and weighed 292 pounds. Accompanied by a friend, he had just stolen a box of Swisher Sweets cigars from a nearby convenience store, and shoved a clerk who'd tried to stop him. The two of them were making a slow getaway, walking down the center of a heavily travelled street.

Arriving at the scene in his car, police officer Darren Wilson stopped and ordered the pair off the street. Brown reached through the window of the vehicle for Wilson's gun, a struggle ensued and Brown was hit in the hand. He fled, pursued by Wilson. Then Brown stopped, turned and charged the officer, who opened fire, killing his massive, enraged attacker in self-defense.

These were the indisputable facts, amply confirmed by both by video and eyewitness testimony. A federal investigation would eventually clear Wilson of civil rights violations, and a grand jury would refuse to indict.

But the facts were of zero consequence to the black and radical white activists who quickly seized on the tragedy, or to a media eager to present Brown as a "gentle giant" and take as gospel the claim of his friend that, far from attacking the officer, Brown had been attempting to surrender when he was shot. In the streets demonstrators endlessly shouted, "Hands up, don't shoot," as the nation was again caught up in a racial maelstrom ginned up by race industry groups like the New Black Panthers and International ANSWER. Jesse Jackson showed up in Ferguson, as did Al Sharpton.

So, too, did Eric Holder, who soberly told the press, "My visit to Ferguson affected me greatly. I had the chance to meet with the family of Michael Brown. I spoke to them not just as Attorney General, but as a father with a teenage son myself. They, like so many in Ferguson, want answers.... We will continue to investigate this shooting, and to help the community work toward healing. And we will continue the conversation this incident has sparked about the need to build trust between law enforcement officers and the communities they serve; to use force appropriately; and to ensure fair and equal treatment for everyone who comes into contact with the police."

Apparently dissatisfied with initial findings showing Brown had been shot in the front, not the back as the mob claimed, Holder also demanded a new autopsy of Brown.

Later, when Wilson was formally exonerated, the attorney general seized the occasion to slam Ferguson's police department for "racial bias both implicit and explicit" and declared it guilty of offenses against citizens that often "blatantly cross the line."

His boss, Barack Obama, struck the same divisive note, emphasizing that "there are still problems and communities of color aren't just making these problems up. Separating that from this particular decision, there are issues in which the law too often feels as if it is being applied in discriminatory fashion... these are real issues. And we have to lift them up and not deny them or try to tamp them down." In fact, as the grand jury testimony showed, the black eyewitnesses on the scene had pointedly backed up Officer Fergurson's testimony. Obama was making up problems.

Though, as always, his language and tone were studiously moderate, his message was all but indistinguishable from that of the activists raging through the streets of Ferguson: that in an irredeemably racist America, resistance is not only understandable, but natural.

Ferguson would prove a turning point in the steep decline of American culture and race relations. In its wake, the Black Lives Matter movement, which had begun organizing in the aftermath of the Trayvon Martin case, turned into a fundraising behemoth – "a money-hoovering operation," as the estimable Roger Kimball termed it, "camouflaged as an angry but high minded form of racial activism" – and would soon emerge as a full-fledged threat to public order.

Nothing would be more associated with the BLM movement than the chant "hands up, don't shoot." A half dozen years later, after the death of George Floyd, as, per Kimball, "Black Lives Matter signs spread like a withering blight across suburbia and scores of millions of dollars poured into the coffers of the activist-cum-entrepreneurs running the organization – the same iconic words would drive protesters and rioters ripping up cities across the country. Even today, "Hands Up, Don't Shoot" remains a magical incantation for BLM protesters.

And from its inception in Ferguson, it was a damnable lie.

CHAPTER 15

THE WAR ON FAITH

Despite Obama's use of religion when it suited his purposes, starting with his joining Jeremiah Wright's church to burnish his credentials with underclass blacks, once he was on the national stage his contempt for the religiously devout became ever more apparent.

The earliest and still most obvious example was his infamous citing of "religion" – before a group of fellow sophisticates in what he supposed was a private session – as one of the false comforts to which their more benighted countrymen clung "as a way to express their frustrations."

So contrary was this sentiment to not only the norms of American political discourse but basic respect for others that his opponent Hillary Clinton, (though she assuredly believed the same) instantly saw the size of the political opportunity at hand. "I was taken aback by the demeaning remarks Senator Obama made about people in small-town America," she declared, with her inimitable brand of faux sincerity. "His remarks are elitist and out of touch."

That they surely were. But of course, what she couldn't say, or perhaps even recognize, (any more than could those in the media covering the story, since they likewise agreed with him), was that Obama's view was a clear echo of Karl Marx's famous dictum: "Religion is the opium of the people."

Indeed, within the tribe of leftist sophisticates to which Obama has always belonged, religious faith is a sure marker of backwardness and ignorance, akin to a belief in fairies and goblins. And the idea that the hicks should impose their backward beliefs on their betters, as they attempt to do on social issues like abortion and gay marriage, is nothing short of infuriating.

What also naturally goes unsaid is that, for all their ready derision of the primitivism of the rubes, progressives genuflect to a higher power of their own – government – and pay strict obeisance to such satellite deities as "science" and "social justice." Theirs is a religion that is in fact the antithesis of the term as others understand it, one grounded not in traditional morality or even a set of fixed values, but governed instead by an ever-evolving set of "certitudes" on everything from the weather to human sexuality.

This is the religion Obama's mentors wished upon America – and, to a startling degree, the one he delivered.

Michael Walsh, the gifted author of *The Devil's Pleasure Palace*, surprised even a sympathetic interviewer, when he characterized the force feeding of cultural Marxism into the mainstream by progressives as "satanic."

"Surely the left isn't *satanic*," objected the other.

To the contrary, countered Walsh, "today's left is the very embodiment of the small-s satanic. The tern applies to the left's advocacy of things that our culture used to recognize as antithetical to moral society, from the nature of American government down to the social issues – some of which weren't even issues a few decades ago. Further, the left has cast aside much of the mufti it was forced to adopt in the United States – 'tolerance' being its principal mask – and can finally be seen for what it really is, a totalitarianism masquerading as beneficence. If that isn't satanic, I don't know what is."

This fundamental remaking of America's cultural understandings had been, of course, ongoing for some time, having accelerated exponentially during the Sixties, but it was under Obama that hostility to traditional morality was weaponized by government. Never had its *diktats* been so blatantly and unapologetically aimed at crushing individual conscience.

This was never more so than in the feds' imposition of the president's most cherished initiative, Obamacare. With a truly jaw-dropping indifference to traditionalist sensibilities, Obama produced a law that explicitly mandated that those running religiously affiliated charities, hospitals and colleges *must* offer contraceptive services in violation of their most deeply held beliefs.

"This is not just about health care," spelled out the lawyer for the Catholic monks at North Carolina's Belmont Abbey College, "This is really about government coercion of religious individuals and institutions."

Even NPR quoted a leading Catholic scholar as describing Obama's as "the most secularist administration in history," and a bishop calling it an "a-theocracy."

Bill Donohue of the Catholic League for Religious and Civil Rights noted that, indeed, the administration's blunt tactics reflected Obama's own evident contempt for the religiously committed, pointing out that on his first Christmas in the White House, he'd actually sought to have the White House's traditional manger scene replaced by a "more inclusive" and "non-religious Christmas." Although that plan was scotched under political pressure, the White House Christmas tree that year included ornaments depicting drag queens and Mao Zedong.

Nor, added Donahue, was the episode out of character. "Given his mindset," he said, "it is not surprising that Obama is opposed to the posting of the Ten Commandments on public property. More surprising are his reservations regarding the display of religious symbols on private property. He was only in office a few months when his advance team told officials at Georgetown University that they had better put a drape over any religious symbols that might appear as a backdrop to where the president was going to speak. To drive the point home, they made sure that the IHS symbol, a monogram of the name Jesus Christ, was not in sight."

On September 15, 2009, Obama gave what was to be a perfunctory speech at the Congressional Hispanic Caucus Institute's 33rd Annual Awards. But he stunned many in the audience when, quoting the Declaration of Independence, he dropped its crucial reference to Americans having been "endowed by the creator" with our inalienable rights.

"What Obama said was no accident; the remarks were prepared," noted Donohue. "Moreover, even after being roundly criticized for this startling omission, Obama did the exact same thing only a month later at a fundraiser in Rockville, Maryland.

"The fact is Obama is uncomfortable with America's Christian heritage. In 2010 he could not bring himself to utter the words 'In God We Trust' when speaking in Indonesia about our national motto; instead, he substituted 'E Pluribus Unum.' But he is quite comfortable with atheists. In 2010, Obama became the first president in U.S. history to welcome a gathering of atheists: administration officials met with activists from the Secular Coalition for America, an umbrella group that includes American Atheists and other virulently anti-Christian organizations."

Little surprise, then, that the ostensible legal fight over Obamacare was in fact an all-out war over what kind of country we were going to be.

In its attempt to bring to heel the Christian owners of Hobby Lobby, the Green family, the Obama Justice Department argued in federal court that the abortion-inducing Morning After pill it insisted the company include in its insurance coverage was a "treatment," claiming that the very act of forming a corporation to engage in commerce constituted a surrender by the owners of their First Amendment right to the free exercise of religion. The DOJ further argued that the government had the power to force individuals to act against their most deeply held beliefs as long as the coercive law is neutral and fairly applied—meaning, that though Obamacare had the effect of persecuting devout Christians, that had not been its specific intent, so the government should be allowed to continue using it to persecute Christians.

Need it be said that this was exactly the opposite of the stance Obama's regime took toward favored groups? Attorney General Holder unhesitatingly described his mission at Justice as *increasing* the civil rights protections of people of color; and it was a given that the merest hint of discriminatory effect against a community of color was likely to bring a strong federal response.

Against the power of the federal government, the religious community continually turned to the courts. In *Burwell v. Hobby Lobby*, the Supreme Court ruled Obamacare's contraceptive mandate violated privately held, for-profit corporations' right to religious freedom. And though it took seven years, the Little Sisters of the Poor's rights of conscience were likewise finally vindicated by the High Court. So, too, though to a lesser degree, would be the principled bakers and florists who'd been massively targeted by progressives for refusing to commit their labors for gay weddings.

Through it all, Obama's war against believers continued apace, as in ways large and petty he and his minions sought to undercut traditional Christianity and its hold on American life and culture.

A key element in that attack was the administration's determination to remake a military that has traditionally drawn a high percentage of its personnel from America's most religious precincts, especially in the South.

The military being an institution over which the president, as commander-in-chief, exercises a great degree of control, while not being subject to great oversight, Team Obama from the beginning made a point of weeding from the ranks practicing Christians as likely racists and oppressors.

What kind of military man did Obama's military no longer want?

Well, for example, there's Navy chaplain Wes Modder.

A Navy chaplain for 15 years following four years in the Marines, Modder was known for his strict adherence to his Pentecostal faith, so when, in 2015, a group of sailors sought him out for spiritual counsel on certain types of personal conduct, including homosexuality and pre-marital sex, he expressed his view that such conduct was immoral.

It was a set-up. Looking to kill his career, the sailors complained of his "backwardness" up the line. The commander of Naval Nuclear Power Training Command, Capt. Jon Fahs, sent a memo to Navy Personnel Command suggesting three different courses of action that the Navy might take against Modder in response to his "homophobia."

The result: Modder was sent before a board of inquiry, where it was concluded he was "unable to function in the diverse and pluralistic environment." He received a "detachment for cause" letter on February 27, 2015.

The quasi-good news was this: When word got out about Modder's ordeal, more than 100,000 Americans signed a petition to Congress on his behalf, and he became a potential political problem. He ended up being exonerated and was allowed to retire honorably a couple of years later.

Which is to say that in the midst of Obama's assault on religion and traditional values generally – indeed, in his wholesale remaking of cultural norms – you took your victories where you could get them.

The result of the Obama policies was exactly what you'd expect: a military better prepared to spout p.c. nonsense than to assault a beach; a military that in terms of competence, was in every way a mere shadow of its former self. But the administration deemed that a small price to pay for an officer corps that welcomed trans leadership and otherwise walked the diversity walk.

As the DOD's Advisory Committee on Diversity and Inclusion in the Armed Services boasts, among other steps to ensure equity, today's military has committed to:

- Training to detect and respond appropriately to bias – both conscious and unconscious. Service members and leaders are also receiving training on recognizing and understanding the impact of their own biases and prejudices.

- Reviewing hairstyle and grooming policies for racial bias.
- Training for commanders on guiding discussions on discrimination, prejudice and bias.

Unsurprisingly, across all the armed services, recruitment is dramatically down, both in numerical and quality terms. In fact, the American miliary today is reduced to taking just about anyone, so long as he/she/they can fog a mirror without quoting Scripture to do it.

In the Navy, things have gotten so bad that in May 2023, amid news it had fallen more than 8,000 short of its recruitment goals, the service was excoriated for publicizing a drag queen as one of its recruitment ambassadors.

This is not to suggest there was not sometimes significant push-back. America remains a deeply religious nation, its greatness inextricably tied to its faith, and there were times Obama was forced to face that fact even on his home turf.

The National Prayer Breakfast is one of those Washington traditions which usually flies below the radar. Held annually in a hotel ballroom in the nation's capital, it is an opportunity for the town's elite to mingle for a bit in a wholesome, politics-free way before another day of grueling fund-raising and lobbying.

But under Barack Obama, on at least a couple of occasions, the NPB became something else: an opportunity for those of faith to directly challenge the man leading the assault on America's faith-based traditions.

In 2012, the event's keynote speaker was author Eric Metaxas, and he delivered a *tour de force*. Politely, but with great conviction, he indicted Obama's views on abortion and other social issues as blatantly anti-Christian. "Who do we say is not fully human today?" Metaxas asked the audience – which also included Joe Biden and Nancy Pelosi. "… those of us who know the unborn to be human beings are commanded by God to love those who do not yet see that."

Metaxas stole the show and left Obama to give a speech full of his usual platitudes about how Christianity included essentially the same moral framework as Hinduism or Islam, a notion that had been decisively repudiated minutes before.

A year later, Obama's moral stewardship of the nation was again challenged at the same NPB, this time even more directly, by Ben Carson, at the time still known only as a highly successful surgeon with a remarkable success story: a black man who had grown up in the Detroit slums in circumstances far more challenging than any middle-class kid in Honolulu. At the NPB, Carson spoke movingly of the existential dangers political correctness posed to America, emphasizing the mortal threat posed by rampant "moral decay" and "fiscal irresponsibility." He further challenged the notion of systemic racism, insisting that in America, anyone could rise through hard work and purpose of will. As for Obama's signature legislative achievement, the Affordable Care Act, such was Carson's scorn that the event's organizers afterward heard from the White House that Obama had taken great offense and demanded an apology.

It was not forthcoming.

Two years later, at the 2015 Prayer Breakfast, Obama had new reason to be embarrassed – but this time not by the rebuke of a religious conservative, but by his own words; a speech so tone-deaf and condescending that it infuriated not only millions of his countrymen, but observant Christians everywhere.

It began as a dissertation on the bloodthirsty Islamic State, but soon lapsed into the moral equivalency typical of his worldview, yet in this case unmatched by his previous public utterances. Insisting that the use of religion to justify murderous violence "is not unique to one group or one religion," he added: "Lest we get on our high horse and think this is unique to some other place, remember that during the Crusades and the Inquisition, people committed terrible deeds in the name of Christ…In our home country, slavery and Jim Crow all too often was justified in the name of Christ."

Needless to say, he failed to mention fact that while Islamic terrorism raged unabated, Christianity, for all its depreciations in the distant past, had long since cleaned up its act; or that while slavery was still commonplace in the Islamic world, it was practicing Christians who a century and a half ago led the fight to banish it in the West and fought to stop it in the predominantly Islamic lands of East Africa and the Indian Ocean.

While *Time* Magazine typified the mainstream media response – noting approvingly that his remarks had been aimed at "so-called believers who are so full of themselves and so confident they are right that that they cast aside all humility. They think that God speaks only to them" – religious Christians erupted in outrage.

It was, said one of them, former Virginia GOP governor Jim Gilmore, "the most offensive speech I've ever heard a president make in my lifetime." It was proof, he added, "that Mr. Obama does not believe in America or the values we all share."

But by now, that was not even close to news.

CHAPTER 16

OBAMA'S RED GUARD

On September 8, 2009, fewer than eight months into his first year as president, Barack Obama did something no other president had done before. During the school day, he gave a speech to children as they sat in their classrooms.

Delivered at noon EST from the auditorium of Arlington, Virginia's Wakefield High, it was watched by a captive audience of 56 million kids nationwide.

Though the speech was largely platitudes about the importance of education and the need to work hard, what had more than a few parents worried – some of them demonstrating outside the school as he spoke – was that Obama's purpose was far from benign. His Department of Education had drawn up lesson plans to accompany the speech, the one for the younger children (K-6) urging them to "write letters to themselves about what they can do to help the president," a suggestion right out of the authoritarian strongman playbook.

And in the lesson plan for grades 7-12, the DOE urged teachers to read aloud from Obama's speeches on education and ask their charges "Why does President Obama want to speak with us today? How will he inspire us? How will he challenge us?"

Moreover, for all its innocuous wording, the speech itself took for granted that his audience shared his ideological assumptions and goals. As he closed his speech, he told the kids, "You'll need the knowledge and problem-solving skills you learn in science and math to cure diseases like cancer and AIDS, and to develop new energy technologies and protect our environment. You'll need the insights and critical-thinking skills you gain in history and social studies to fight poverty and homelessness, crime and discrimination, and make our nation more fair and more free…"

In short, in its way it was even more ominous than candidate Obama's earlier scornful comments about working class desperate clingers: now, from the nation's bully pulpit, Obama was coming for the kids.

Jim Greer, chairman of the Florida Republican Party, rightly termed the speech "an invasive abuse of power," intended to "indoctrinate America's children to his socialist agenda." Conservative commentator Tammy Bruce mockingly called it "Make September 8 Parentally

Approved Skip Day," tweeting, "You are your child's moral tutor, not that shady lawyer from Chicago."

"The thing that concerned me most about it was it seemed like a direct channel from the president of the United States into the classroom, to my child," the *New York Times* quoted Brett Curtis, a father from Pearland, Texas, who'd kept his three children home that day. "I don't want our schools turned over to some socialist movement."

And, of course, that was exactly Obama's purpose.

Since his days organizing on Chicago's South Side, he had worked to bring the idealistic young to the cause, knowing, as radicals always have, how vital it is to hook them into social justice early.

In the recent presidential campaign, his pitch to young people had been passionate and full-throated. "I want you to go out and talk to your friends and talk to your neighbors," he declared as the 2008 race neared its finish. "I want you to talk to them whether they are independent or whether they are Republican. I want you to argue with them and get in their face."

The result was what the *Christian Science Monitor* termed a "seismic generational shift in American politics." Obama carried fully two-thirds of voters under thirty.

As the *Monitor* noted, the Obama campaign used "tech-savvy tactics that elude older generations...(T)hey sent text messages, blogged, instant-messaged, posted YouTube videos, designed Obama iPhone applications, and mobilized online support for the man who represents two things that young people thrive on: hope and change...

".... In many primary states, the organization began at the high school level, with local 'Barackstars' groups formed to bring supporters together. The Obama campaign created a campaign social networking site (MyBO) where young people could communicate, plan their own activities and become involved in the campaign. Then, when the primary day approached, they merged this campaign with old-fashioned door-to-door canvassing."

Doddering John McCain, meanwhile, didn't know how to use a Blackberry.

But if the media's coverage of his campaign's outreach to the young was overwhelmingly positive, in the *Wall Street Journal* Stanley Kurtz countered with a piece suggesting what a President Obama would likely have in mind for the nation's schools. The piece looked back on Obama's much hidden relationship with ex-Weatherman and now educational reformer Bill Ayers, and their work together on the Chicago Annenberg Challenge. "The CAC's agenda," he wrote, "flowed from Mr. Ayers's educational philosophy, which called for infusing students and their parents with a radical political commitment, and which downplayed achievement tests in favor of activism... External partners like the South Shore African Village Collaborative and the Dual Language Exchange focused more on political consciousness, Afrocentricity and bilingualism than traditional education... The point, says Mr. Ayers in his (book) *Teaching Toward Freedom,* is to 'teach against oppression,' against America's history of evil and racism, thereby forcing social transformation."

And, indeed, now that Obama was in the Oval Office, his team moved decisively to put key elements of that radical agenda into practice. Most notably, there was Secretary of Education Arne Duncan's infamous 2014 "Dear Colleague Letter" on school discipline. Dispatched to school superintendents across the country, it warned that racial disparities in suspension rates would be grounds for finding school districts in violation of federal anti-discrimination law, and therefore at risk of losing federal funding.

As the Manhattan Institute's Max Eden wrote, though cast as a "guidance," the directive "in fact formalized a fundamental shift in the Department of Education's approach to civil rights enforcement... The school system of Broward County, Fla., led the nation in promoting and implementing this policy shift and served as the exemplar for President Barack Obama's directive. Broward's efforts to end the 'schoolhouse-to-jailhouse pipeline' by reducing in-school arrests for drug, assault and weapons charges were celebrated by racial-justice and criminal-reform advocates around the country.

"But it was precisely this preference for social justice over safety that allowed Nikolas Cruz, the Marjory Stoneman Douglas High School shooter, to avoid arrest in Broward County, despite years of criminal behavior on school grounds and countless red flags regarding his unstable and psychopathic personality.

"What was the response to the horror of the Parkland mass shootings? Not that the lenience shown toward Cruz be curtailed. Instead, it was renewed demands for gun control."

The standard of equal outcomes promulgated by the Obama Dear Colleague Letter, Eden noted, "was the basis for hundreds of bad-faith investigations conducted with the express purpose of forcing school districts to adopt the leniency policies pioneered in Broward County. School districts were presumed guilty and unable to prove themselves innocent; the only way these 'investigations' could end was for school districts to agree to the Department of Education's policy demands."

The Education Secretary was right "that African American students are the subjects of school discipline at higher rates than white students," noted Gail Heriot, a conservative holdover on the U.S. Civil Rights Commission. "Although he did not mention it, it is also true that white students are the subjects of school discipline at higher rates than Asian American students, and that male students are disciplined at higher rates than female students." Moreover, she added, "by failing to consider the other side of the coin — that African-American students may be disproportionately victimized by disorderly classrooms — its policy threatens to do more harm than good even for the group Secretary Duncan was trying to help… school discipline is important and… the Department of Education's policy has contributed to the problem of disorderly classrooms, especially in schools with high minority student enrollment."

Another of the Obama DOE's Dear Colleague letters, this one from its Office of Civil Rights, was directed at colleges and universities. An outright sop to radical feminists, it relied on the activists' fraudulent statistics that one in five women is sexually assaulted during her college years. This was the reasoning it used to direct administrators, under the authority of Title IX, the federal statute prohibiting sex discrimination (originally intended to guarantee women equal access to participation in sports) to crack down on sexual assault cases or risk loss of their federal funding.

The letter read: "If a school knows or reasonably should know about student-on-student harassment that creates a hostile environment, Title IX requires the school to take immediate action to eliminate the harassment, prevent its recurrence, and address its effects."

The result was the creation at colleges throughout the nation of vast new bureaucracies, that in turn set up Star Chamber proceedings in which men accused of sexual impropriety were presumed guilty and often suffered dire consequences, including expulsion, with nothing remotely resembling due process. In a preview of the MeToo movement, the horror stories ran rampant.

Later, to her credit, Trump Education Secretary Betsy DeVos rolled back the rules and provided more just treatment of the accused. But upon taking over, Biden's Department of Education immediately reinstated the Obama regulations, this time with modified language to include sexual orientation and gender identity for LGBTQI+ students.

While by the time of Obama's presidency, the nation's colleges and universities were already largely inhospitable to conservative thought, they had not quite become the snake pits of vicious ideological conformity we see today. Indeed, the nation was shocked, in a way it certainly would no longer be today, by a 2016 video of a scene at Yale that showed the sorry state into which that supposed bastion of intellectual life had lately fallen.

The episode had been touched off by a letter to the student body shortly before Halloween from the school's Intercultural Affairs Council asking that they show cultural sensitivity in their choice of costumes. The letter was so silly, that a professor named Erika Christakis, decided to reply, writing in essence, *C'mon, let's let the kids have a little fun.* "Is there no room anymore for a child or young person to be a little bit obnoxious… a little bit inappropriate or provocative or, yes, offensive?" she asked. "American universities were once a safe space not only for maturation but also for a certain regressive, or even transgressive, experience; increasingly, it seems, they have become places of censure and prohibition."

What happened then was that this completely reasonable notion set the very students the professor was trying to help into paroxysms of rage. They insisted Yale was a "safe space" and accused Christakis of threatening that coddling academic womb. And when her husband, also a professor at the school, tried to engage a mob of them in civil conversation – this part was the part on videotape – they got in his face, screaming vile epithets.

For millions of ordinary Americans, watching the scene on their computers, this was something entirely new. Yes, they'd been hearing for a while about the spoiled Participation Trophy Generation, and about how many overindulged adult children were retreating to their parents' basements rather than leading lives and forming families of their own.

But this was something different. This was students at one of America's allegedly premiere educational institutions, supposedly our best and brightest and destined to lead the country into the future, acting out against professors with vile words and physical aggression; radicals primed to overturn the system, and not giving a damn who knew it, because they knew consequences would not be forthcoming.

This was the generation nurtured by eight years of Barack Obama.

Of course, today no one would be the least bit surprised by such behavior, as it is so widely accepted that our leading colleges and universities do less teaching than indoctrinating. As the veteran conservative commentator (and ex-leftist radical) David Horowitz observes, "The source of our current ills – the lawlessness in our streets, the destruction of our borders, the racist 'equity' policies of the Democrat Party, the "woke" derelictions of our military leaders, can all be traced to the indoctrination of our educated classes in hatreds spawned by cultural Marxism."

It's all there in the stats:

- 61 percent of Americans aged 18-24 today have a positive reaction to the word "socialism," compared with 58 percent reacting positively to the word "capitalism."
- Eight in 10 college students supported the BLM race riots. (BLM activists were themselves likely to have college degrees, and many campuses serve as organizing centers for the movement.)
- A 2022 survey of college students revealed that 78% believe "systemic racism is a major problem in our society," and 50% believe "America is inextricably linked to white supremacy."
- A New York Times poll showed that only 26% of Democrat voters with a bachelor's degree agreed that America is the greatest country in the world. Only 12% of Democrats 18-29 believed that America was the greatest nation.
- 57% of the liberal students, (as opposed to 12% of conservative students) reported that college classes make them not proud to be Americans. 61% of the liberals, (and 16% of the conservatives) say they instill a negative view of capitalism.
- A 2022 survey of recent Harvard graduates reveals just 4% are conservative, down from 7% when they entered. 55% support the Green New Deal, 54% want to eliminate border security, and 33% back BDS, the terrorist-sponsored boycott of Israel.

All this is the product of a university system in which 82% of the faculty are leftists, 16% are moderates and only 1.4% are conservatives.

As the writer Daniel Greenfield sums it up: "Universities have become efficient indoctrination centers that couldn't be any more destructive if they were being run by China and Russia... Generations are emerging who are not merely liberal, but support criminals and racists, and the destruction of America."

To be sure, some young people – including those who've escaped to these shores from actual totalitarianism – see that clearly. A defector from North Korea named Yeonmi Park writes scornfully of her Columbia classmates that they're "living in the freest country you can imagine, and they're saying they're oppressed? It doesn't even compute. I was sold for $200 as a sex slave in the 21st century under the same sky. And they say they're oppressed because people can't follow their pronouns they invent every day?"

"I grew up in a communist country," echoes a young letter writer to the *New York Times,* "and I am well aware of the flavors and threats of a totalitarian system. What is happening on campuses in the US and in the society at large has all the elements of what the communist ideologues used to do. First, proclaim that you are fighting for a just cause (and name a cause that does seem to be just at face value), e.g., rights of exploited workers or oppressed minorities. Then institute unquestionable 'truisms' and label any discussion about their merits as 'reactionary' and 'extremist.' Start by indoctrinating the most malleable group – the youth. Finally, introduce serious adverse consequences for those 'heretics' questioning the orthodoxy, which will cow the vast silent majority."

All serious students of history know this, particularly students of the 1960's Chinese Cultural Revolution, which our current woke collegiate tyranny so closely resembles. Yet on campuses where systemic racism and climate change are obsessions and many can't date the American Revolution to within 50 years – insistence on history and facts is itself a micro-aggression.

In today's colleges and universities, Barack Obama might no longer be in the coddled students' daily thoughts, but he is their spiritual father. Having unleashed his vision on the world, it is self-perpetuating, and fueled by those who came of age under his sway.

Today George Soros's Open Society lavishly funds a virtual army of Gen-Z activists; "foot soldiers," as the New York Post observes, "on behalf of abolishing border enforcement, defunding cops and ending cash bail," and the accounts of "young influencer activists" are "littered with White House and far-left talking points." "We are unequivocally supportive of Medicare for all, the Green New Deal, Palestinian Liberation (and) a plethora of progressive policies that a vast majority of Gen-Z supports," Gen-Z for Change founder Aidan Kohn-Murphy proclaimed on (Chinese owned) TikTok, while the group's 24-year old deputy director, Victoria Hammett, inflames her 800,000-plus, overwhelmingly female followers with reports of 13-year old rape victims being forced by pro-lifers to carry their babies to term.

"Why the fuck did you accept the position?!" screamed an infuriated young black woman at Yale in 2016, inches from the shocked face of a white professor old enough to be her father. "Who the fuck hired you?"

One can only wonder where she is now.

Perhaps she joined with BLM, the Marxist outfit born in the wake of Ferguson, which won such widespread respectable support post-George Floyd. Obama's own daughters took part in BLM protests, and he proudly declared them "so much wiser, more sophisticated and gifted than I was at their age."

Or maybe that young woman's rage led her to align with Antifa, that other tip of the activist spear, offering even more immediate opportunity to build the new society by torching buildings and assaulting cops.

But most likely, and in its way more chilling, like most students from elite colleges, and others also, she's today waging the revolution from the inside. For today there are multiple paths the young may take to commit social justice, through academia, media, Hollywood the corporate world, even within the realm of sports.

When conservative Judge Kyle Duncan of the Fifth Circuit Court of Appeals was invited to address Stanford University's Law School's Federalist Society in March 2023, he was famously silenced by a mob of future lawyers and judges, not to mention a dean who supported their obnoxious outbursts. The piece he wrote for the *Wall Street Journal* about the experience was appropriately titled "My Struggle Session at Stanford Law School," because it's obvious and clear the universities are indeed building the Red Guard in America. The only question now is whether there's any way back to the functional society that Obama and his lickspittles have torn away. For, if not, who can doubt that America's enraged young would be capable of perpetrating such horrors?

CHAPTER 17

THE UNDERMINING OF DONALD TRUMP

"Organizing for Action (OFA), a group founded by former President Barack Obama and featured prominently on his new post-presidency website, is distributing a training manual to anti-Trump activists that advises them to bully GOP lawmakers into backing off support for repealing Obamacare, curbing immigration from high-risk Islamic nations and building a border wall," reported conservative investigative journalist Paul Sperry on February 17, 2017.

The tactics set down in the playbook were quite specific, Sperry noted, drawn from Obama's own experience as a community organizer. For instance, it "advises protesters to go into halls quietly so as not to raise alarms, and 'grab seats at the front of the room but do not all sit together,' "to make it seem like the whole room opposes the Republican host's positions…It also urges them to ask hostile questions — while keeping 'a firm hold on the mic' — and loudly boo the GOP politician… giving a platform to pro-Trump authoritarianism, racism, and corruption.'"

Thus, noted Sperry, less than a month into Donald Trump's presidency, using such methods, OFA had disrupted Republican meeting and town halls nationwide.

"After the event," the manual goes on, "protesters are advised to feed video footage to local and national media. Unfavorable exchanges caught on video can be devastating [when] shared through social media and picked up by local and national media."

The manual provides a script leftists can use in calls to media "to complain: 'I'm honestly scared that a known racist and anti-Semite will be working just feet from the Oval Office … It is everyone's business if a man who promoted white supremacy is serving as an adviser to the president.'"

That Obama was personally behind this campaign to undermine his successor is not a matter of speculation. He all but bragged about it. Following Trump's upset victory the previous November, writes Sperry, Obama had "personally rallied OFA troops to 'protect' his legacy in a conference call. 'Now is the time for some organizing,' he said. 'So don't mope" over the election results.

"He promised OFA activists he would soon join them in the fray. 'Understand that I'm going to be constrained in what I do with all of you until I am again a private citizen, but that's not so far off,' he said. 'You're going to see me early next year, and we're going to be in a position where we can start cooking up all kinds of great stuff.'

"Added the ex-president: 'I promise you that next year Michelle and I are going to be right there with you, and the clouds are going to start parting, and we're going to be busy. I've got all kinds of thoughts and ideas about it, but this isn't the best time to share them.

"'Point is, I'm still fired up and ready to go, and I hope that all of you are, as well.'"

At the time, Organizing for America, founded by Michelle in 2013 and run by ex-Obama officials, had more than 250 offices nationwide, its ranks swelled by more than 32,000 organizers – i.e. Obama's Red Guard – with another 25,000 actively in training. These last, wrote Sperry, "go through a six-week training program similar to the training — steeped in Alinsky agitation tactics — Obama received in Chicago when he was a community organizer."

Their aim, in concert with other Obama loyalists, was straightforward: to destroy the Trump presidency, and stigmatize Trump supporters as morally beyond the pale. Because they succeeded, we are still suffering the consequences.

The four years Donald Trump occupied the Oval Office were both a time of achievement – rapid economic growth and energy independence at home, peace and renewed projection of American strength abroad – and a period of bitterness and tribal hatreds unprecedented in the modern era. One was the fruits of the Trump presidency. The other was the subversive work of Obama's shadow third term, carried out by Obama political operatives aligned with a Deep State overwhelmingly staffed and led by Obama true believers.

Yet, almost without exception, those on the left still believe even the biggest of the big lies the Obamites propagated to bring Trump down: not the Russia Hoax in all its permutations but, arguably even more destructive, that the 45th president's supporters are white supremacists.

Having initially been caught short by Trump's 2016 victory, the Obama's forces quickly recovered, reacting quickly and savagely. What they brought about was nothing less than a rolling political *coup d'état* against an American president.

On the covert side, too, it began before the election. Clinton lawyer Mark Elias realized that in the highly unlikely event Hillary lost, with Obama still in the White House, he could count on weaponized federal intelligence and law enforcement agencies to push the tawdry smears concocted by opposition research outfit Fusion GPS, via washed-up British spy Christopher Steele, about Trump and Russia. The most brazen of these was that he'd hired a pair of Moscow hookers to urinate on a bed Obama had slept in.

Once the comically implausible Steele dossier had been successfully fed into the system, the Obama-groomed federal bureaucracy was able to keep Trump's administration on the defensive until the very end.

The 300-page Durham Report, when it finally appeared in May 2023, would lay out the particulars in staggering and sickening detail.

Special counsel John Durham had been hired back in 2020, following two years of investigations which failed to unearth any proof the president had colluded with Vladimir Putin to beat Hillary Clinton. His task was to get to the bottom of the weaponization of the intelligence and law enforcement communities.

From the executive summary of the Durham report, herein the genesis of the FBI's Crossfire Hurricane investigation which created the Trump-Russia affair:

In the spring of 2016, Perkins Coie, a U.S.-based international law firm, acting as counsel to the Clinton campaign, retained Fusion GPS, a U.S.-based investigative firm, to conduct opposition research on Trump and his associates. In mid-May 2016, Glenn Simpson of Fusion GPS met with Steele in the United Kingdom and subsequently retained Steele and his firm, Orbis Business Intelligence ("Orbis"), to investigate Trump's ties to Russia. Steele described himself as a former intelligence official for the British government and was also at the time an FBI CHS [Confidential Human Source]. Beginning in July 2016 and continuing through December 2016, the FBI received a series of reports from Steele and Orbis that contained derogatory information about Trump concerning Trump's purported ties to

Russia. ...Steele provided the first of his reports to his FBI handler on July 5th. These reports were colloquially referred to as the "Steele Dossier" or "Steele Reports."

As noted, it was not until mid-September that the Crossfire Hurricane investigators received several of the Steele Reports. Within days of their receipt, the unvetted and unverified Steele Reports were used to support probable cause in the FBI's FISA applications targeting [Carter] Page, a U.S. citizen who, for a period of time, had been an advisor to Trump. As discussed later in the report, this was done at a time when the FBI knew that the same information Steele had provided to the FBI had also been fed to the media and others in Washington, D.C.

In particular, one allegation contained in an undated Steele Report, identified as 2016/095, described a "well-developed conspiracy of co-operation" between Trump, his campaign, and senior Russian officials. This allegation would ultimately underpin the four FISA applications targeting Page. Specifically, the allegation stated:

Speaking in confidence to a compatriot in late July 2016, Source E, an ethnic Russian close associate of Republican US presidential candidate Donald TRUMP, admitted that there was a well-developed conspiracy of co-operation between them and the Russian leadership. This was managed on the TRUMP side by the Republican candidate's campaign manager, Paul MANAFORT, who was using foreign policy advisor, Carter PAGE, and others as intermediaries. The two sides had a mutual interest in defeating Democratic presidential candidate Hillary CLINTON, whom President PUTIN apparently both hated and feared.

And this was the conclusion of the Durham report where the Trump-Russia affair is concerned...

Based on the review of Crossfire Hurricane and related intelligence activities, we conclude that the Department and the FBI failed to uphold their important mission of strict fidelity to the law in connection with certain events and activities described in this report. As noted, former FBI attorney Kevin Clinesmith committed a criminal offense by fabricating language in an email that was material to the FBI obtaining a FISA surveillance order. In other instances, FBI personnel working on that same FISA application displayed, at best, a cavalier attitude towards accuracy and completeness. FBI personnel also repeatedly disregarded important requirements when they continued to seek renewals of that FISA surveillance while acknowledging - both then and in hindsight - that they did not genuinely believe there was probable cause to believe that the target was knowingly engaged in clandestine intelligence activities on behalf of a foreign power, or knowingly helping another person in such activities. And certain personnel disregarded significant exculpatory information that should have prompted investigative restraint and re-examination.

Our investigation also revealed that senior FBI personnel displayed a serious lack of analytical rigor towards the information that they received, especially information received from politically affiliated persons and entities. This information in part triggered and sustained Crossfire Hurricane and contributed to the subsequent need for Special Counsel Mueller's investigation. In particular, there was significant reliance on investigative leads provided or funded (directly or indirectly) by Trump's political opponents. The Department did not adequately examine or question these materials and the motivations of those providing them, even when at about the same time the Director of the FBI and others learned of significant and potentially contrary intelligence.

Durham was too polite in not attributing the obvious motives for the shady FBI investigation into the Trump campaign.

For it was clear that the motive was political animus. That was made glaringly obvious, if it wasn't before, by the obnoxious screeching on cable news outlets like MSNBC by the likes of FBI gumshoes Andrew McCabe and Peter Strzok, who authorized and led Crossfire Hurricane, respectively.

The Deep State was weaponized against Trump before he even entered the 2016 presidential race. Members of Obama's law enforcement agencies so hated the new president that more than a few of these Deep State operatives actually believed the sludge contained within the Steele Dossier, notes former Justice Department attorney Andrew McCarthy.

"Even if the Justice Department and the FBI could not prove Steele's allegations, at least not yet," McCarthy writes, "they still believed that Trump was compromised and that the Russians could be blackmailing him. So we arrive at the knotty question for Obama political and law-enforcement officials: How do we 'engage with the incoming team' of Trump officials while also determining that 'we cannot share information fully as it relates to Russia?' How do we assure that an investigation of Trump can continue when Trump is about to take over the government?"

The answer was obvious – and so much the better that it fit with Obama's long-established contempt for democratic norms. Although out of power, he'd continue to work his will via surrogates, with the FBI and intelligence services fully on board for behind-the-scenes dirty work. "By the time he left office on January 20, 2016," as investigative journalist Jack Cashill puts it, "Obama had all his cucks in a row – prominent sycophants in every branch of the government and in every major newsroom prepared to ruin Donald Trump's presidency in service to a lie."

"He weaponized information and showed a willingness to lie," one of those surrogates, former Obama Deputy National Security Advisor Ben Rhodes writes in his memoir "using traditional media like television, and new media platforms like Twitter, Facebook, and YouTube, to spread disinformation into open, Western societies like a virus."

Only in a classic case of projection, Rhodes was talking about Putin, not his old boss.

Notes Cashill dryly, "I imagine Obama reading this and saying, 'Vladimir, hold my beer.'" Of course, Rhodes would later admit that he had fabricated many of the claims he made about his work undertaken for the American people as a negotiator with Iran, which is perhaps not surprising as he has master's degree in fiction writing.

By far the Obama team's greatest coup at the onset of Trump's presidency was the FBI's takedown of the new president's national security advisor, General Mike Flynn. A Trump loyalist and committed ideological conservative in an administration otherwise overstaffed by traditional Republicans with no allegiance to their new boss, (often the opposite), Flynn had been explicitly targeted for destruction.

"What is our goal?" asked Bill Priestap, the then-counterintelligence director at the FBI, in a hand-written note to a colleague, immediately before a scheduled interview with Flynn, "Truth/Admission or to get him to lie, so we can prosecute him or get him fired?"

It was the latter. Questioned, without his lawyer present, about contacts he'd had with the Russian ambassador – standard diplomatic practice for a soon-to-be national security advisor – Flynn was caught, and prosecuted, on a minor discrepancy. He was gone before he'd even started.

From the Obamite perspective, such tactics needed no justification. With Trump having run for president on a full repudiation of the substance and style of everything Team Obama stood for, he and his people had to be crushed. He'd chosen America's country class over its ruling class, repeatedly calling out the latter for its terrible record of neglect and scorn of ordinary Americans.

He had no use for politesse or political correctness. And he'd promised to "drain the swamp."

This was read as what it was: a declaration of war. Trump, perhaps naïve to a fault, had no idea what he was unleashing. For the Obama mode of war was: By Any Means Necessary.

Moreover, Team Obama began with key advantages. Beyond bedrock support (and a corresponding hatred of Trump) in the media, there was the deep reservoir of hostility toward the new president on the part of much of the public, a matter as much of his style as his substance. Prior to the election, Obama had declared that electing Trump would be "an insult to my legacy," which it very much was, and this was the rare post-election period that brought no cool-down in political temperature. Interviewed in *Rolling Stone,* Obama changed his story, saying that it was false that the election represented a repudiation of his tenure, insisting he'd have beaten Trump if he hadn't been term-limited. Trump had only won, he said, because of *"Fox News* in every bar and restaurant in big chunks of the country."

For his part, White House spokesman Josh Earnest spent the post-election week trashing the president-elect and pushing the narrative of Russian interference being responsible for his victory. In short, softening up the public for the more vicious charges to come.

Obama lent credence to the Russian interference tale by officially sanctioning Russia for its "election interference" and expelling 35 Russian diplomats in retaliation.

Next came a report by Obama's Department of Homeland Security alleging that the Russians had hacked the Democratic National Committee's e-mail server – something which despite massive media efforts, would never be proven. (In fact, independent media investigators used technical data from leaked emails and other files to show it was more likely the servers had been downloaded to a portable drive not transferred over the internet – which put them under the jurisdiction and control of the Department of Homeland Security. This was itself illegal, as the federal government has no authority to confiscate state voting systems.)

All of it served to build the narrative that the 2016 election – and Trump's victory – were illegitimate.

For those who cared to notice, it was becoming increasingly clear Obama had enabled Secretary of State Clinton in genuinely corrupt behavior – from the routine mishandling of highly classified material to the all-but-open bribery of the

Clinton Foundation in the Uranium One deal – that should have made her unelectable in the first place.

"Make no mistake, in protecting Hillary, Obama was also protecting the entire administration," as Matt Margolis and Mark Noonan write in *The Worst President In History*, their book covering the largely unreported sleaziness of the Obama years. "Hillary would guarantee Obama's legacy would be preserved. Donald Trump ran on promises to undo Obama's legacy and see that justice would be done regarding Obama-era corruption."

As the formal certification of Trump's victory approached, the Clinton campaign and the Democratic National Committee put out the word to their activists to harass Trump electors, demanding they "go faithless" and refuse to vote for him. Wholly unprecedented, the tactic had no chance of success, but it had the effect of ramping up the partisan animus even further. It is also ironic in that federal authorities would later arrange for an indictment against Trump for conspiracy to encourage electors to be faithless – the very crime that Obama's followers had openly engaged in during the final weeks of 2016.

Regardless, by the time of Inauguration Day, January 20, 2017, a vast mob of "leftists" called forth by the "community organizing" universe had descended on the nation's capital, many masked and dressed in the black garb that would soon come to be identified with Antifa. Free lodging and other support had been arranged for them in advance, as was the legal representation it was assumed they would need.

Tellingly, of the more than 200 violent protesters arrested in Washington on Inauguration Day, not one was sentenced to a single day in jail. "Solidarity was what won the case," crowed Sam Menefee-Libey, of the DC Legal Posse activist collective. "I hope that organizers and people on the left study it."

Worldwide an estimated two million people protested Trump's inauguration, among them half a million marching in front of Trump Tower in New York. The next day saw half a million more on the streets in Washington's vaunted Women's March, many chanting, in what would prove to be considerable understatement, "Welcome to your first day, we will not go away!"

The Resistance, as it was already being proclaimed, would go on, unabated and unchallenged – indeed, widely celebrated – for the next four years.

Throughout 2017, as the Trump administration tried to find its footing, it found itself paralyzed by non-stop media claims that the Russians engineered his election. So fully were the media and Congressional Democrats invested in this narrative, that Trump, expecting he would be quickly exonerated, made the colossal error of agreeing to appoint a special prosecutor – meaning that over the next two years, the likes of CNN and MSNBC (and to an only slightly less insane degree, the *New York Times* and *Washington Post*) were able to joyously, endlessly guess at when he'd have to resign in disgrace, if not be frog marched off to prison.

Before you could say "fake news," Special Prosecutor Robert Mueller had built a team full of Hillary Clinton partisans to attempt to railroad the president. And by the time the investigation finally came up dry, exonerating Trump of "colluding" with Russia, incalculable damage had been done.

Having suffered a disastrous 2018 midterm election, the GOP's hold on the House of Representatives was gone, and with Nancy Pelosi back in the Speaker's chair, such key Trump legislative goals as undoing Obamacare in favor of market solutions to runaway healthcare costs were dead.

But there was so much more. Obama had put in place hundreds of last-minute punitive regulations which left tens of billions of dollars of business capital on the shelf. He'd taken in thousands of unvetted "Syrian" refugees, most of whom turned out to be not from Syria but elsewhere in the inflamed Muslim world. And when Trump thus declared a moratorium on accepting suspect refugees from eight Islamic nations, an Obama-appointed federal judge in Hawaii issued an injunction to stop him.

More often than not, when Trump tried to undo something Obama had done with his "pen and phone," as his famous boast about bypassing the duly elected Republican Congress had it, there was an Obama-appointed judge playing super-legislature to stop him.

Obama, still in Washington, D.C. after leaving office, violated another key ex-presidential custom by refusing to shut up about politics.

When Trump moved to tear up the Paris Climate Accords, for example, rightly characterizing them as a global-warming-related international giveaway that would greatly limit America's productive capacity, Obama scolded that "The tradition has been you carry [international agreements] forward across the administrations" – failing to note that Paris was an "executive agreement," not a treaty, so it had never been ratified by the Senate, or was otherwise governed by the force of any precedent, nor was it legally-binding. Nonetheless, for carrying through a campaign promise most Americans wanted him to keep, Trump was widely condemned as lawless.

The four-year war was unrelenting. Before 2017, nobody in America had heard the word Antifa. By the time Trump left office thanks to virtually non-stop political violence and aggressive demonstrations, everybody had.

It was a straightforward campaign of intimidation.

"Let's make sure we show up wherever we have to show up," Congresswoman Maxine Waters of the slums of Los Angeles shouted to supporters through a bullhorn. "And if you see anybody from that Cabinet in a restaurant, in a department store, at a gasoline station, you get out and you create a crowd. And you push back on them. And you tell them they're not welcome anymore, anywhere."

It was a message the entire left took to heart.

Prominent conservative figures like Fox News host Tucker Carlson and Trump press secretary Sarah Huckabee Sanders found themselves hounded and harassed at restaurants. Then it was ordinary people who were set upon by demonstrators screaming about perceived racial, sexual or economic injustices. Morons with bullhorns and primitive weapons disrupted events, and not just political ones, in major cities around the country. A general sense of brewing chaos covered the ground like new snow.

And in May of 2017, when the city of Charlottesville, Virginia decided to remove the statue of Confederate general Robert E. Lee, the resulting protest was seized upon by the left and its media allies to cheap-shot Trump and his voters – i.e., half the country – as "white supremacists."

It would be the left's foundational Biggest Lie, enthusiastically spread and uncritically embraced, and it splintered the country as never before, establishing as fact among tens of millions a smear that henceforth had been regarded as plausible only among rage-blind leftist activists.

Crucially, the Charlottesville protest was meant to be peaceful. The demonstrators had secured a permit. It aimed to make the rather tame point that historical landmarks and monuments should not be levelled because the history they mark is inconvenient, even if that history is for many repugnant; for, indeed, the Taliban might have used the same justification for its defenestration of the ancient Bamiyan statues that caused worldwide outrage.

Many ordinary citizens were on hand for the protest, as well as others far less savory, including white nationalists bearing tiki torches and chanting "You will not replace us!" They staged a night-time march through the city the night before the planned protest, and as objectionable as the marchers were, their demonstration was peaceful. But when the word got out about that march, the left showed up the next day in droves to counter-protest.

Without a permit, and with weapons.

In the melee that ensued, a young woman was run over by a car driven by one of the "alt-right" crowd, and all hell broke loose. A national crisis was trumpeted by the Usual Suspects in the media, and all eyes turned to Trump – who was now supposed to make an Obamaesque statement of "racial healing" – never mind that in almost every instance, those presidential statements had been akin to throwing kerosene on a bonfire.

Trump's first statement noted that he was short on facts but that he abhorred violence. And then, a couple of days later, he held a press conference at Trump Tower to tout a plan to streamline the nation's Byzantine infrastructure approvals process – only to find himself set upon by the White House press corps, demanding condemnation of "his" people and approbation of those on the other side.

Here's a partial transcript of how it went...

> **REPORTER**: *The CEO of Walmart said you missed a critical opportunity to help bring the country together. Did you?*
>
> **TRUMP**: *Not at all. I think the country -- look, you take a look. I've created over a million jobs since I have been president. The country is booming, the stock market is setting records, we have the highest*

employment numbers we've ever had in the history of our country. We are doing record business. We have the highest levels of enthusiasm, so the head of Walmart, who I know, who's a very nice guy, was making a political statement. I mean, I would do it the same way, you know why? Because I want to make sure when I make a statement that the statement is correct. And there was no way – no way – of making a correct statement that early. I had to see the facts, unlike a lot of reporters, unlike a lot of reporters.

I didn't know David Duke was there. I wanted to see the facts. And the facts, as they started coming out, were very well-stated. In fact, everybody said his statement was beautiful. If he would have made it sooner, that would have been good. I couldn't have made it sooner, because I didn't know all of the facts. Frankly, people still don't know all of the facts. It was very important – excuse me, excuse me. It was very important to me to get the facts out and correctly. Because if I would have made a fast statement and the first statement was made without knowing much other than what we were seeing. The second statement was made after it with knowledge, with great knowledge. There are still things – excuse me. There are still things that people don't know. I want to make a statement with knowledge, I wanted to know the facts, okay.

REPORTER: Two questions: was this terrorism? And can you tell us how you are feeling about your chief strategist Steve Bannon?

TRUMP: I think the driver of the car is a disgrace to himself, his family and this country. And that is – you can call it terrorism, you can call it murder. You can call it whatever you want. I would just call it as the fastest one to come up with a good verdict. That's what I'd call it. And there is a question. Is it murder? Is it terrorism? Then you get into legal semantics. The driver of the car is a murderer, and what he did was a horrible, horrible, inexcusable thing.

REPORTER: Can you tell us how you are feeling about your chief strategist, Mr. Bannon? Can you talk about that?

REPORTER: Steve Bannon --
TRUMP: I never spoke to Mr. Bannon about it.

REPORTER: Can you tell us broadly about – do you still have confidence in Steve?
TRUMP: Well, we'll see. And look, look, I like Mr. Bannon. He is a friend of mine, but Mr. Bannon came on very late. You know that. I went through 17 senators, governors and I won all the primaries. Mr. Bannon came on very much later than that, and I like him. He is a good man. He is not a racist – I can tell you that. He is a good person, he actually gets very unfair press in that regard. We'll see what happens with Mr. Bannon.

He's a good person, and I think the press treats him frankly very unfairly.

REPORTER: *They have called on you to defend your national security adviser H.R. McMaster against these attacks.*

TRUMP: *I did that before. Senator McCain? Senator McCain. You mean the one that voted against Obamacare? Who is Senator McCain? You mean Senator McCain who voted against us getting good health care?*

REPORTER: *Senator McCain said that the alt-right is behind these attacks, and he linked that same group to those that perpetrated the attack in Charlottesville.*

TRUMP: *Well, I don't know. I can't tell you. I'm sure Senator McCain must know what he is talking about, but when you say the alt-right, define alt-right to me. You define it. Go ahead. Define it for me, come on, let's go.*

REPORTER: *Senator McCain defined them as the same group.*

TRUMP: *Okay, what about the alt-left that came charging at [indiscernible] – excuse me – what about the alt-left that came charging at the, as you say, the alt right? Do they have any semblance of guilt?*

REPORTERS YELL INDISTINCTLY

TRUMP: *What about this? What about the fact that they came charging – they came charging with clubs in their hands swinging clubs? Do they have any problem? I think they do.*

REPORTERS YELL INDISTINCTLY

TRUMP: *As far as I'm concerned, that was a horrible, horrible day. Wait a minute, I'm not finished. I'm not finished, fake news. That was a horrible day.*

REPORTERS YELL INDISTINCTLY

TRUMP: *I will tell you something. I watched those very closely, much more closely than you people watched it. And you had, you had a group on one side that was bad. And you had a group on the other side that was also very violent. And nobody wants to say that, but I'll say it right now. You had a group – you had a group on the other side that came charging in without a permit, and they were very, very violent.*

REPORTER: *Do you think what you call the alt left is the same as neo-Nazis?*

TRUMP: *Those people – all of those people, excuse me – I've condemned neo-Nazis. I've condemned many different groups, but not all of those people were neo-Nazis, believe me. Not all of those people were white supremacists by any stretch.*

REPORTER: *Well, white nationalists –*

TRUMP: *Those people were also there, because they wanted to protest the taking down of a statue Robert E. Lee. So – excuse me – and you take a look at some of the groups and you see, and you'd know it if you were honest reporters, which in many cases you're not. Many of those people were there to protest the taking down of the statue of Robert E. Lee. So this week, it's Robert E. Lee, I noticed that Stonewall Jackson's coming down. I wonder,* *is it George Washington next week? And is it Thomas Jefferson the week after? You know, you really do have to ask yourself, where does it stop?*

REPORTERS YELL INDISTINCTLY

TRUMP: *But, they were there to protest – excuse me – you take a look the night before, they were there to protest the taking down of the statue of Robert E. Lee. Infrastructure question. Go ahead.*

REPORTER: *Does the statue of Robert E. Lee stay up?*

TRUMP: *I would say that's up to a local town, community or the federal government, depending on where it is located.*

REPORTER: *Are you against the Confederacy?*

REPORTER: *On race relations in America, do you think things have gotten worse or better since you took office with regard to race relationships?*

TRUMP: *I think they've gotten better or the same – look – they have been frayed for a long time, and you can ask President Obama about that, because he'd make speeches about it. I believe that the fact that I brought in, it will be soon, millions of jobs, you see where companies are moving back into our country. I think that's going to have a tremendous positive impact on race relations. We have companies coming back into our country. We have two car companies that just announced. We have Foxconn in Wisconsin just announced. We have many companies, I'd say, pouring back into the country. I think that's going to have a huge, positive impact on race relations. You know why? It is jobs.*

What people want now, they want jobs. They want great jobs with good pay. And when they have that, you watch how race relations will be. And I'll tell you, we're spending a lot of money on the inner cities – we are fixing the inner cities – we are doing far more than anybody has done with respect to the inner cities. It is a priority for me, and it's very important.

REPORTER: Mr. President, are you putting what you're calling the alt-left and white supremacists on the same moral plane?

TRUMP: I am not putting anybody on a moral plane, what I'm saying is this: you had a group on one side and a group on the other, and they came at each other with clubs and it was vicious and horrible and it was a horrible thing to watch, but there is another side. There was a group on this side, you can call them the left. You've just called them the left, that came violently attacking the other group. So you can say what you want, but that's the way it is.

REPORTER: You said there was hatred and violence on both sides?

TRUMP: I do think there is blame – yes, I think there is blame on both sides. You look at, you look at both sides. I think there's blame on both sides, and I have no doubt about it, and you don't have any doubt about it either. And, and, and, and if you reported it accurately, you would say.

REPORTER: The neo-Nazis started this thing. They showed up in Charlottesville.

TRUMP: Excuse me, they didn't put themselves down as neo-Nazis, and you had some very bad people in that group. But you also had people that were very fine people on both sides. You had people in that group – excuse me, excuse me. I saw the same pictures as you did. You had people in that group that were there to protest the taking down, of to them, a very, very important statue and the renaming of a park from Robert E. Lee to another name.

REPORTER: George Washington and Robert E. Lee are not the same.

TRUMP: Oh no, George Washington was a slave owner. Was George Washington a slave owner? So will George Washington now lose his status? Are we going to take down – excuse me. Are we going to take down, are we going to take down statues to George Washington? How about Thomas Jefferson? What do you think of Thomas Jefferson? You like him? Okay, good. Are we going to take down his statue? He was a major slave owner. Are we going to take down his statue? You know what? It's fine, you're changing history, you're changing culture, and you had people – and I'm not talking about the neo-Nazis and the white nationalists, because they should be condemned totally – but you had many people in that group other than neo-Nazis and white nationalists, okay? And the press has treated them absolutely unfairly. Now, in the other group also, you had some fine people, but you also had troublemakers and you see them come with the

black outfits and with the helmets and with the baseball bats –
you had a lot of bad people in the other group too.

REPORTER: *I just didn't understand what you were*
saying. You were saying the press has treated white nationalists
unfairly?

TRUMP: *No, no. There were people in that rally, and I*
looked the night before. If you look, they were people protesting
very quietly, the taking down the statue of Robert E. Lee. I'm
sure in that group there were some bad ones. The following day,
it looked like they had some rough, bad people, neo-Nazis, white
nationalists, whatever you want to call 'em. But you had a lot
of people in that group that were there to innocently protest and
very legally protest, because you know, I don't know if you know,
but they had a permit. The other group didn't have a permit. So
I only tell you this: there are two sides to a story. I thought what
took place was a horrible moment for our country, a horrible
moment. But there are two sides to the country.

From this – herein presented in full – the media narrative
instantly became that Trump defended the "alt-right," the
white nationalist crowd, and even the neo-Nazis, and it was
a brazen, provable lie. It was obvious to anyone who cared
about the truth that what he was defending was the mainstream, permitted protesters seeking to make the case against
erasing historical landmarks, a point of view which until
recently was the consensus. Robert E. Lee had long been
an exemplar of character and decency for Americans across

regions and spanning the ideological spectrum, especially in regard to his work in calling for an end to the devasting war in which he'd played such a key part.

But of course, none of that was part of the conversation promoted by the media in the wake of Charlottesville. Over and over, the "good people on both sides" clip was trotted out as evidence the Nazis had been, in effect, stand-ins for Trump as his supporters.

"Trump blows up damage control as he blames 'both sides' for Charlottesville," as POLITICO had it.

And in this narrative the Antifa thugs were the heroes.

Thus, Trump – who before running for office had won awards from the likes of Jesse Jackson and Al Sharpton – was now cast as the epitome of the modern bigot, and "neo-Nazis" henceforth included anyone who opposed the taking-down of iconic statues; and by extension, soon enough, opposed the radical left's seizure of American history in general.

Trump's bombastic and caustic manner obviously didn't help. But he wasn't the instigator, and he could not have made his position any clearer.

Except to the media. At every turn, the media regarded the actual violence of "The Resistance" (Antifa and Black Lives Matter) as legitimate speech. Trump's speech, however, was violent.

The left's Biggest Lie continues to do its insidious work today, smothering the possibility of honest conversation on a vast range of subjects which progressives desperately want left unexamined, from the mutilation of our young through transgender surgery to the reintroduction of segregation and race hatred in the seductive guise of "equity."

Post-Charlottesville, throughout the remainder of the Trump years, Antifa and Black Lives Matter would continue to play the role they'd performed to such widespread media approval on that terrible day just four months into his term. Appearing on the streets in force and battle gear, their aim would be to shut down all opposition to the socialist agenda moving at breakneck speed into every aspect of American life.

Black Lives Matter, born on Obama's watch after the Trayvon Martin fiasco, turned during the Trump years into a massive cultural and political juggernaut. Far from an organic phenomenon, it was the product of old-fashioned Saul Alinsky community organizing, cheer-led from the start by the nation's community-organizer-in-chief, with his endless reminders of America's problematic racial history. As he summed it up in 2015, "the African American community is not just making this up," as if anyone had ever suggested such a thing. Obama's gambit was the same as BLM's: to play down the extraordinary racial progress the country had made, and to seize every opportunity to declare white racism deep and intractable.

With Obama having set the stage, especially in his exploitation of the Ferguson riots and his shameless promotion of the out-of-control-cops narrative, the chaos wrought by George Floyd's 2020 death would present the radical left with a gift priceless even beyond their most reckless dreams.

In a healthy society, even the horrific circumstances of Floyd's death would have been properly cast as a cautionary tale of the terrible fate of those who ignore the time-tested rules for a meaningful life. A violent criminal and drug addict, he'd ingested three times the fatal dose of fentanyl before attempting to pass some bad paper at a Minneapolis convenience store. And while the video of rogue Minneapolis cop Derek Chauvin kneeling on Floyd for almost nine minutes is agonizing to watch, his death was almost surely due more to Chinese-made fentanyl than out-of-control cops.

Either way, ultimately no one was more responsible for George Floyd's life and death than George Floyd.

Yet in the America with the racial climate bequeathed by Barack Obama, that wasn't how it worked. Floyd became the victim of all victims – and not just a victim of the cops involved, but of America itself.

The bonfire that had been so scrupulously prepared, was suddenly aflame. Instantly, Antifa and BLM were on the streets of the nation's largest cities, faces covered and armed with street fighting gear, their grand unified field theory of racist, oppressive America enjoying the vast newfound support of deluded millions.

Minneapolis went first. It was followed by almost every other major city with arson and looting night after night, in place after place. Millions in damages, then tens of millions, most of it in minority communities. In Seattle, Antifa actually cordoned off a chunk of downtown and called it an "autonomous zone" ruled by a drug dealer, and CHAZ, the

Capitol Hill Autonomous Zone, quickly became a hellscape devoid of food, water and electricity, while Seattle's useless far-left Democrat mayor, Jenny Durkan, did nothing. Rage ruled the streets. Not hope, and certainly no brotherhood or reason. They didn't want those.

Democrat politicians, recognizing the damage they were doing to Trump's reelection prospects as the anti-cop, pro-BLM narrative took hold, only egged the rioters on. California Senator Kamala Harris contributed to a bail fund for "protesters." "This is a movement, I'm telling you," she explained to a sympathetic Stephen Colbert. "They're not going to stop. And everyone beware because they're not going to stop. They're not going to stop before Election Day in November, and they're not going to stop after Election Day. And that should be — everyone should take note of that, on both levels, that they're not going to let up, and they should not, and we should not."

In fact, the George Floyd riots were more about culture than about politics. They were the left's long-sought excuse to institute "fundamental change" in the ways Americans spoke, thought and were permitted to behave. For here, in the horrifying video, was the ultimate, inarguable proof of America's systemic racism.

As if to drive home the point, Barack Obama, more than three years out of office, weighed in, inveighing that for millions of black Americans "being treated differently on account of race is tragically, painfully, maddeningly 'normal...whether it's while dealing with the health care system, or interacting with the criminal justice system, or jogging down the street, or just watching birds in the park."

The last two references were, respectively, to Ahmaud Arbery, a Georgia black man who'd been killed while jogging three months earlier, and to a much publicized recent event in New York's Central Park when a privileged white woman called the police about a black man who'd told her to leash her dog.

Systemic racism, indeed!

Michelle Obama, for her part, chimed in with: "I'm exhausted by a heartbreak that never seems to stop. Right now it's George (Floyd), Breonna (Taylor), and Ahmaud. Before that it was Eric, Sandra, and Michael. It just goes on, and on, and on."

White liberals got the message. Thus, for a couple of weeks, it was trendy for upscale suburban protestors to lie prone in the street for 8 minutes and 46 seconds – the period Derek Chauvin knelt on George Floyd's neck. And so did the institutions they controlled. Overnight:

- Corporate America went fully woke, mandating race-based quotas and paying untold millions in blood money to Black Lives Matter and affiliated organizations.

- Cancel culture took hold, ruling free thought on the subject of race so illicit that even the phrase All Lives Matter was grounds for termination in the work place.

- Efforts to "Defund the Police" demoralized law enforcement in departments nationwide.
- American history itself was under siege, as schools were renamed, and more statues of illustrious figures were brought crashing down; this was soon followed by unapologetic leftist proselytizing in school textbooks.
- Standards of all kinds were denounced as symbols of white supremacy, and done away with, along with laws on the books deemed to unduly affect black lawbreakers.

This, of course, is only a very partial accounting of the vast damage to the quality of and substance of daily life in America triggered by the George Floyd killing. All that need be said is that, in its violent aftermath, there appeared a best-selling picture book for toddlers entitled *Antiracist Baby*.

Is this the America Barack Obama wanted in his calls for fundamental change? This is the wrong question. What mattered is that the old America had to be destroyed for his to be built.

Donald Trump had cast himself as the defender of that older America, and in the mayhem of the George Floyd summer, with his hoped-for reelection date approaching, the left did what it took to make sure he'd have no second term.

In fact, heading into the final year of his term, by every objective standard Trump had seemed poised for reelection. On his watch, the economy was in liftoff mode; domestic energy production had risen to levels not even imagined just a few years before; his tax cuts had repatriated trillions of dollars in investment capital which had, thanks to Obama's IRS, been parked overseas.. There'd been huge foreign policy wins as well. The Abraham Accords began the process of normalizing Israel's relations with several Arab countries. Our enemies in Iran were weaker, frightened and more constrained. Russia was pulling back many of its covert operations in Ukraine. Perhaps most notably, before the pandemic America's trade deficit with China had declined by $200 billion per year.

Yet by the time of the Floyd mayhem, Trump was of course also dealing with the COVID-19 pandemic – another epoch-shaping crisis his political enemies quickly harnessed to their own ends.

The Democrat Party, which belonged to Obama lock, stock and barrel, played COVID to the hilt. And in Dr. Anthony Fauci and White House Coronavirus Response Coordinator Dr. Deborah Birx, they had the perfect collaborators on the inside, committed and highly motivated political actors passing (and celebrated in the media) as reputable and public-spirited scientists. In a time of widespread public grief and panic, they seemed to offer desperately needed good sense and calm rationality. Indeed, in retrospect, theirs was a joint performance worthy of any of the awards their narcissistic friends in Hollywood hand out to one another with such abandon. A Lifetime Achievement award, maybe, for selfless service beyond the call of duty to the Deep State and the Democratic Party!

They certainly had Donald Trump fooled.

Both would prove invaluable as the election approached, making sure that the president under whom they supposedly served regularly came off as incompetent and out of control.

An Obama Deep State holdover, Birx all but admitted as much in her 2022 memoir.

Meanwhile, as the entire sentient world knows by now when Trump suggested that the common antiviral hydroxychloroquine might be of use in fighting the infection – in fact, it would later prove to prevent hospitalization in 80-90 percent of COVID cases if taken early – Birx allowed the president to become an object of media ridicule, as the drug was widely derided as useless if not harmful. This despite some 75 years of widespread use in battling any number of viral infections.

Soon enough, Birx' public health bureaucracy put the hammer on the drug entirely, with pharmacists all over the country refusing to fill prescriptions for HCQ (as well those for the similarly derided, and also effective, ivermectin), under threat of losing their licenses.

"After the heavily edited documents were returned to me," wrote Birx, of those in the White House with whom she was supposedly working to craft public messaging, "I'd reinsert what they had objected to, but place it in those different locations. I'd also reorder and restructure the bullet points so the most salient—the points the administration objected to most—no longer fell at the start of the bullet points. I shared these strategies with the three members of the data team also writing these reports. Our Saturday and Sunday report-writing routine soon became: write, submit, revise, hide, resubmit.

"Fortunately, this strategic sleight-of-hand worked."

As the entire sentient world knows by now, Fauci long dismissed even the possibility that Covid had emerged from China's Wuhan lab – until it came out in February 2023 that the supposedly disinterested clinician had had both a professional and personal financial investment in suppressing the truth all along. That's when it emerged that the "scientific paper" he had used as evidence to debunk the Wuhan lab theory three years earlier had, in fact, been commissioned, edited and re-edited by none other than Fauci himself. Yet, with an audacity that would do any Mafia don proud, he'd stood beside Trump at the White House and calmly described the paper as the work of "a group of highly qualified evolutionary virologists" who'd determined that the origin of the pandemic was "in bats as they evolve and the mutations that it took to get to the point where it is now is totally consistent with a jump of a species from an animal to a human."

Through it all, for over three years, Fauci and his hatchet woman likewise squelched dissenting voices within their domain – in other words, actual scientists, doing their jobs. Dr. Scott Atlas, a Trump appointee to the COVID task force, argued early on against alarmism and lockdowns, challenged the efficacy of masks, and advocated for herd immunity and the reopening of schools. Birx so effectively undercut him that he resigned in November 2020.

Former Centers for Disease Control and Prevention Director Dr. Robert Redfield would later testify he too had been "sidelined" from internal debates at the outset of the pandemic when he tried to make the case for the lab leak theory. "I let them know as a virologist that I didn't see that this was anything like SARS or MERS" – prior outbreaks that had originated in animal wet markets.

But Fauci, he said, was having none of it. "This was a prior decision that there's one point of view out there, and anyone who doesn't agree with it is going to be sidelined."

Needless to say, the devastation of the American economy during an election year was, for Democrats, a happy consequence of the pandemic.

But the final (or at least the decisive) nail in Trump's electoral coffin was the use of COVID as the Democrats' pretext for wanton abuse of the electoral process, especially in highly competitive states. In Pennsylvania, for example, the state's constitution says that any changes in voting procedures must be approved by the legislature. But, using COVID as an excuse, the state's Democratic governor unilaterally re-wrote the state's voting laws to allow voters to use drop-boxes and not to bother going to vote in their local precincts. This permitted widespread ballot harvesting and a heavy reliance on mail-in votes. That meant that a huge proportion of the counted votes came from people who were never identified. These added votes likely proved to be the difference in the state, helping Biden win in Pennsylvania.

In an atmosphere where Democrats were forever screaming about threats to democracy, and had already once impeached Trump for imagined crimes, with another to come, this was the real thing, in spades, and stark evidence of how dramatically, and quickly, the country had changed that almost no one on the left was willing to say so.

Certainly, none of the Democrats, who were both the manufacturers of the corruption, and its beneficiaries spoke up. Yet, as recently as 2005, three years before Obama was elected president, such silence would have been unthinkable. That was the year the bi-partisan Carter-Baker Commission – co-chaired by Democrat former president Jimmy Carter and Republican former secretary of state Jim Baker – issued its findings on the crucial matter of protecting election integrity.

"Elections are the heart of democracy," it began. "If the elections Americans use to select our leaders are defective," it continued, "democracy is in danger."

The report went on to make a series of best-practices recommendations agreed upon by both sides as the gold standard the country should shoot for.

- A national system to connect state and local voter registration lists
- Voter identification based on a universally available REAL ID card
- Policies to improve voter access for all communities, as well as innovations like vote centers and voter information lookup sites

- Stronger efforts to combat fraud, especially in absentee voting
- Auditable paper backups for all voting technology

The Carter-Baker commission also called for an end to ballot harvesting. And one of its strongest recommendations was to avoid mail-in balloting at all costs.

Needless to say, by 2020 – in fact, since the Obama presidency – not only was the adoption of common-sensical measures to ensure election integrity a pipedream, but such measures were sure to be denounced as racist. And in a number of key states where they had already been implemented in state law, COVID was used as a pretext for their elimination.

Was the 2020 election stolen via electronic means or vote harvesting or any of a variety of progressive machinations? Very likely. But what is certain beyond even a scintilla of doubt is that the Dems saw to it that it that every conceivable means of theft was possible, pre-fixed by law going forward.

You don't have to buy the idea the election was stolen in the literal sense. You're allowed to; whether through irregularities in the counting machines or through old-fashioned stuffing of ballot boxes thanks to the work of harvesters paid for through some $400 million in funding from Facebook founder Mark Zuckerberg and his wife via a shadowy outfit called the Center for Tech and Civic Life, the irregular tactics employed by the Democrats in that election came on a scale never before seen and their vetting was nonexistent.

But even if you don't believe the ballot-harvesting and the mules and the strange delays in vote-counting amounted to theft, there was one unmistakable Obama-style dirty trick which ruined the 2020 election as an accurate measure of the temperature of the American electorate.

The Hunter Biden laptop story, or more to the point its suppression, might be the single most descriptive and terrifying anecdote in recent American political history, and its effects may have signaled the end of our constitutional republic in anything resembling our founding.

In October of that year, the *New York Post* ran a short series of articles detailing the scandalous, scurrilous and devastating information found in computer files on a laptop that Hunter Biden, son of Obama's vice president and Democrat nominee Joe Biden, had abandoned at a Delaware computer repair shop. Hunter Biden is a drug abuser and sexual miscreant, and video files and still images from the laptop certainly made that clear in titillating fashion. More importantly, it made clear that he's the point man for a Biden family corruption ring which takes influence-peddling to a level even the Clintons would have to bow to.

The laptop opened the door to that corruption scheme, which has since been broken open through the release of bank records that a congressional investigation has produced, and it contained evidence that the Bidens were shaking down foreign actors in places like China and Ukraine in a pay-for-play influence-peddling scheme.

. This was material the FBI had access to for well more than a year because the repair shop owner had turned the computer over to the feds after seeing what was on it. But fearing the exact inaction that would take place, he also turned a copy of the drive over to Trump's attorney Rudy Giuliani.

And that's how the revelations from the laptop turned up in the *New York Post.*

But when the nation's oldest continuously running newspaper published its reports on what was on the laptop, major social media platforms like Facebook and Twitter, on what turned out to be demands from federal bureaucrats as revealed in lawsuits filed by several state attorneys general and in disclosures following Elon Musk's purchase of Twitter, suppressed them. Links to *Post* pieces about the laptop were deleted, and users sharing them were even banned.

Search engines also suppressed stories about the laptop in the runup to the election, making it difficult for people to find information on it.

And other mainstream media platforms were silent about spreading the laptop reports.

What would have been a shocking lack of journalistic interest in, well, journalism was given a fig leaf of respectability thanks to a cabal of Obama hacks working to recapture the parts of the federal government they didn't control during Trump's term. Future secretary of state Tony Blinken, future national security adviser Jake Sullivan and a former Obama-era CIA head named Michael Morrell put together a list of 50 (51, including Morrell) "intelligence community" veterans who denounced the reports of what was on that laptop as "Russian disinformation."

It was a bald-faced lie, one just as obvious as the Trump-Russia collusion narrative had been, but it was enough for partisan Democrat media outlets like CNN, the *New York Times*, the *Washington Post* and others to go silent not just on the laptop but its punitive suppression on social media and the internet.

After the election, several surveys indicated that more than 10 percent of the 81 million Americans who were reported to have voted for Joe Biden would not have done so had they known about the Biden crime family the laptop reports exposed. And for good reason: the Biden presidency is quite possibly the most disastrous in American history, and its corruption is near to total.

Was the 2020 election stolen? That's less a question of fact than of interpretation, much like Obama's rigged state senate election in 1996. What 2020 really amounted to was electoral politics Obama-style.

And we're seeing that is fatal in a republic.

Indeed, over the three years since, under the faux presidency of Joe Biden, the measures necessary to ensure the survival of the increasingly implausible Democratic narrative have grown steadily more draconian; and, arguably even more chilling, have increasingly been applied without so much as the hint of embarrassment. January 6 protesters are locked away with scarcely the semblance of due process in what is rightly termed an American gulag. Free speech is all but criminalized; the "wrong" views on race or even Covid are grounds for loss of career and social opprobrium. As with the notorious laptop, those daring to challenge the narrative are silenced on social media via behind-the-scenes administration pressure on the Silicon Valley behemoths; and once that pressure is revealed, rather than cause an outcry, the revelation is itself buried by a compliant mainstream media.

Above all, casting aside all pretense of concern for the legal niceties, the fully weaponized justice system intensifies its Javert-like pursuit of Donald Trump, despised not just as an individual but as the representative of tens of millions of ordinary Americans; and as if to hammer home the point, simultaneously goes to extraordinary lengths to give a pass to the outright corruption of Biden and his brood.

We used to ask, only semi-seriously, if it could ever happen in America.

Thanks to Obama, it has.

CHAPTER 18

PLEASE, NO, NO FIFTH TERM!

"Barack and I don't do things incidentally," said Michelle Obama in 2018. "There's a strategy."

So when the former First Lady announced in late 2022 that she'd written a second autobiography, following in her husband's multiple-memoir footprints, many wondered what that strategy might be.

For anyone concerned for America's future, the very possibility was terrifying: might Michelle be considering a 2024 presidential run?

"In the promotional interviews for her new book, *The Light We Carry*," as notes Joel Gilbert in *American Thinker*, "Michelle Obama insists that the book is simply her personal 'toolkit' about how she deals with the challenges of 'uncertain times.' No, *The Light We Carry* is not a self-help book. It is Michelle's crafty attempt to position herself to be the Democrat nominee for president in 2024."

He adds that as a classic pre-presidential tome, the "goal of *The Light We Carry* is the same as *Becoming*: to strengthen her appeal to women and minorities, key Democrat party voting blocs. In the first five chapters of *The Light We Carry*, Michelle recounts her journey from Chicago to Princeton University. In Chapter 6, she writes about meeting Barack at her Chicago law firm, going to Hawaii the first time, and their marriage. Chapter 7 is 'Meet my Mom' about how great it was having her Mom living in the White House with them. Chapter 8 is about Michelle's group of friends while she was first lady. Chapter 9 is the White House years and her being a Black first lady, and a lot of talk about daughters Malia and Sasha. The final chapter culminates in a highly political offering called 'Going High', a discussion of Michelle's political "motto" which is 'when they go low, we go high.' Michelle unveiled this saying in a 2016 campaign speech after going low on Donald Trump with a vicious attack excoriating Trump for alleged behaviors she either exaggerated or pulled out of context."

What gave the possibility of a Michelle real plausibility is that an overwhelming majority of Democrats would be thrilled to see it happen – a feeling that has only grown with the sense of looming electoral disaster in November 2024. In a party as bereft of decent ideas as of decency itself, (and, in its perverse racism, locked into a problem of its own making, the need on the ticket for a candidate "of color") the notion of renominating the corrupt husk of an incumbent and his even more deeply unpopular veep – was rightly terrifying. Suddenly even the most reliable Dem media stalwarts were suggesting that, given his "age" – never his glaring cognitive failures, never his appalling personal corruption – he ought to do the noble thing and withdraw from the race. (Some suggested he might simultaneously announce he was pardoning his felonious son, which too would be cast as noble and selfless.)

At the same time, at least one shark, California's oily pretty boy Gavin Newsome, was already circling, even as he continued to earnestly profess support for Biden. But Newsom was less of a sure thing, having so thoroughly wrecked California's quality of life as governor that even some Democrats have reservations about what he might do to the rest of America.

No, Michelle was the obvious choice. Ted Cruz speculated, she might even be "parachuted in" by "Democratic kingmakers" as late as August 2024, on the eve of the party's convention. Such a scenario would also serve the purpose of assuaging the Democrats' core constituency, black women, otherwise deeply committed to Harris.

It is an all-too-real possibility, one that leaves the rest of us left hanging on the hope that, while she has never inspired anything resembling trust in the past, Michelle meant it all those times she spoke of her loathing of politics; and there's also the fact that she's not exactly given to a heavy workload.

In this regard, the best news of late may be that the Germans paid the former First Lady 700,000 euros – $741,000 in real money – for a one hour "speech" repeating the things her ghost writers put in her books. That comes to $12,350 per minute. As president, she would pull down a mere $400,000 per *year*. And she would have to show up. (On the other hand, Joe Biden…)

The spirited conservative commentator Kurt Schlichter noted the threat a Michelle Obama candidacy could pose to the American people – and the likelihood of its success…

"What are the chances that Michelle Obama will come out of her expensive and luxurious retirement to try to take up the banner for the Democrats in 2024? She has certainly sparked a lot of speculation, and a lot of dread, among Republicans. And the Republicans are right to dread her. The kind of Chardonnay – swilling, overly-credentialed, and under-educated, sexually unsatisfied suburban wine women who adore Michelle Obama are going to be a key demographic in 2024, and Michelle owns them lock, stock, and Häagen-Dazs."

Schlichter ultimately concluded that Michelle Obama won't be on the ticket simply because, even if handed the nomination, she'd be reluctant to go through a general election campaign.

Another quick word of prayer that he might prove to be on target!

Because if she goes for it, she won't be easy to take down. Gilbert, for his part, at least suggests a strategy that, should the GOP be smart enough to take it – obviously, a forlorn hope – has at least a shot at success at denting her appeal to the Dems' core constituency: telling the full truth about Mrs. Obama's own dismal record in shamelessly exploiting her fellow blacks. As Gilbert writes in his book *Michelle Obama 2024: Her Real Life Story and Plan for Power*, back when Barack was still a relative political cypher, "Michelle's two most significant jobs in Chicago involved working on behalf of white liberal elites to deal with the problems that Black people were causing them.

"Chicago liberals couldn't hire a White person to make 20,000 Blacks homeless. Their answer was to hire Michelle Obama. She became Mayor Richard Daley's assistant planning commissioner. Her job was to facilitate the destruction of the low-income all-Black Cabrini Green housing project and cede the choice downtown real estate to Democrat party donor developers like Tony Rezko. Nor could the White liberal elites at the University of Chicago Medical Center hire a White person to deny access to health care to Blacks. Only a Black person could fill that job. For a cool $300,000 a year, Michelle was prepared to do all the denying that was needed. Michelle headed up the 'South Side Health Collaborative,' a scheme to prevent Blacks who showed up at the University of Chicago Medical Center emergency room from receiving medical care. Michelle made sure they were put into white vans and shipped to crappy neighborhood strip mall clinics on the South Side.

"Only a Black person could credibly do either of these jobs while telling those turned away, 'This is for your own good.' Why was Michelle Obama so callous toward the Black community in her professional career? The answer is simple: Michelle was never really a part of the Black community in Chicago. She was not even from the 'South Side' of Chicago, as she claimed, but from South Shore, a middle-class community on Lake Michigan."

Still, in America, 2024, the truth has a lot less purchase than it once had, and the more dangerous the facts, the more certain they are to be dismissed by "indignant" leftists and an "outraged" media as white supremacist fiction.

All we can say for sure is that Obama and his team will not surrender power without a fight; that, and that in today's tumultuous political climate, no scenario can be ruled out.

Already the Obamites have succeeded beyond their wildest dreams in their fundamental transformation of America. For more than 14 years he has been the most consequential figure in the country's life and culture, and by now those of us not in on his game are staring slack-jawed at what he and his crew have made of them. But in their eyes, there is yet more to be done.

Future Democrat presidents will certainly try, but none will manage to brand the nation so fully in Obama's image. Barring a run by Michelle, for decades to come his party will pine for comparable another vessel of Hope and Change, as prior generations of Democrats yearned for another FDR, and then another JFK.

So more than ever, it's the job of better Americans to stop them now.

If nothing else, Obama has offered invaluable lessons for those who retain hope for America, if we're smart enough to learn them. And the first of these is the glaring reality that America is no better at socialism than is Russia or Venezuela. In places where Obama and his ilk permanently hold power – Detroit, Baltimore, Chicago, Philadelphia, Newark, New Orleans, Cleveland – the rot is already likely irreversible; and to a shocking degree, much of the rest of country is also largely under their thumbs.

If the leftist insanity is not stopped, there will be no escape from the utter defeat of America.

Through leftist policy and leftist cultural aggression, Obama has thrown our country into deep decline in nearly every way imaginable. Today's Obama-Biden America, burdened by woke-driven regulation and a financial system shackled to ESG and DEI, prospers only haltingly, when at all.

Increasingly, Americans regard the old American Dream as an impossibility – the "bad joke" Frank Marshall Davis sneeringly described it as all those years ago. Today, barely half of us even think capitalism is worth saving.

Militarily we're weaker now than we were before World War II, while our military leadership seems more interested in sex changes for our soldiers than in sustaining our naval strength.

Our freedoms? The left's cultural fascists have perfected ways to silence opposition without resorting to the jackboots and truncheons as in the past – though, if it comes to it, jackboots are hardly out of the question. Ask Matt Houck, the Pennsylvania abortion activist targeted by the federal government for daring to offer sidewalk counseling to pregnant women; or Scott Smith, the Virginia father hauled from a Loudon County school board meeting for protesting the rape of his daughter by a boy in a skirt; or any conservative trying to ply a trade in Hollywood or academia or even a major corporation. Ask even liberal journalists Matt Taibbi or Michael Schellenberger, who dared challenge the mainstream narrative on…freedom.

And it was all so unnecessary. There was never any compelling reason for Obama's election, beyond the sentimental desire on the part of mostly white America to exorcise its demons.

And where are we left after 14 years of Reverend Wright, the New Black Panthers, beer summits, Eric Holder, Trayvon, Ferguson, Ibram X. Kendi, Black Lives Matter, Colin Kaepernick and Ilhan Omar, Critical Race Theory? With most Americans regarding race relations as far more fraught than when Obama came on the scene – and terrified to have anything like an honest conversation on the subject.

Obama and his allies have not merely birthed a militant anti-white racism, they have lent mainstream respectability to its most strident backers in politics, media and corporate

America, weaponizing politics, economics and culture along the way.

That's what Obama and his cabal have brought on us: Decline and despondence. And if you're not on their team, they demand that you get your mind right, as they push the new bigotry even harder, lighting the White House in rainbow colors for Gay Pride Month and lecturing Christians on faith and good works.

On their watch, the very word "patriot" has taken on bad odor among progressives, seen as redolent of "white nationalism." If you're not with them, you're the Other. You will be worn down, demonized and liquidated — politically or otherwise. You're the target of what used to be Alinsky's Rules for Radicals, and is now Democrat dogma.

But we know better – we know that real patriotism is a love of country and all its people.

If America's slide into oblivion is to be halted. a fifth Obama term – whoever the candidate is – must be prevented.

"For the first time in my adult lifetime, I am really proud of my country," declared Michelle Obama in 2008, with her husband on his way to the presidency.

We owe it to future generations to make sure she's never that proud again.